NELSON'S NAVY

Text by
PHILIP HAYTHORNTHWAITE
Colour plates by
WILLIAM YOUNGHUSBAND

First published in Great Britain in 1993 by
Osprey Publishing, Elms Court, Chapel Way,
Botley, Oxford OX2 9LP United Kingdom

Email: info@ospreypublishing.com

© Copyright 1993
Osprey Publishing Limited
01 02 03 04 05 10 9 8 7 6 5 4 3 1

Also published as Elite 48 *Nelson's Navy*

ISBN 1 84176 252 0

Filmset in Great Britain by Keyspools Ltd., Golborne,
Lancashire
Printed in China through World Print Ltd.

FOR A CATALOGUE OF ALL BOOKS PUBLISHED BY
OSPREY MILITARY AND AVIATION PLEASE WRITE TO:

The Marketing Manager, Osprey Direct USA,
PO Box 130, Sterling Heights. MI 48311-0130,
United States of America.
Email: info@ospreydirectusa.com

The Marketing Manager, Osprey Direct UK,
PO Box 140, Wellingborough, Northants, NN8 4ZA,
United Kingdom.
Email: info@ospreydirect.co.uk

VISIT OSPREY AT
www.ospreypublishing.com

FRONT COVER: The Battle of Trafalgar 1805
(Courtesy of The Bridgeman Art Library)

BACK COVER: Horatio Nelson (1758-1805) (Courtesy
of the Ann Ronan Picture Library)

INTRODUCTION

Despite the many celebrated victories of the British Army during the Napoleonic Wars, the role of the Royal Navy should never be overlooked. The 'wooden walls' formed the country's first and most important line of defence, and ranged throughout the world to protect Britain's trade-routes and in support of the land forces and overseas possessions. A verse of the poem *John Bull's Call to the Sailors* by 'Mr. Courteney', published in *The Gentleman's Magazine* in September 1803, could not have been more apposite:

'Britannia, still flourish, exultingly smile,
Fam'd for valour and beauty's sweet charms;
While navies victorious encircle your isle,
Rest in safety, nor dread vain alarms'.

Expenditure on the Royal Navy reflected its importance: between 1800 and 1812 it consumed between a quarter and a fifth of the nation's *entire* annual budget, and only in 1813–15 did this slip to less than one-fifth. In 1800, when naval expenditure represented over one-third of the annual budget, it exceeded the sum spent on the army and at £12,619,000 represented some 46.75 per cent of the entire war effort, including subsidies to allied nations. Naval expenditure rose from £10,211,378 in 1803 to £20,058,412 in 1810, and remained reasonably constant until 1814, reaching a peak of £21,996,623 in 1813, inclusive of £6,568,320 spent on the victualling department, and £565,790 on the transport department.

This expenditure, and the professionalism, training and morale of the Royal Navy produced a service superior to that of any other maritime nation. Statistics published in 1839, relating to the French Revolutionary and Napoleonic Wars, record that 1,209 enemy vessels were sunk or captured as against 166 British, of which the comparative figures for ships of the line were 167:7, and frigates 323:27. Against France the statistics of capital ships (50 guns

Of the various types of combat fought by the Royal Navy, the most famous – but rarest – was the 'fleet action', a pitched battle fought at close range, as in this depiction of the 'Glorious First of June'. (Engraving by A. Le Petit after P. J. De Loutherbourg)

Much more common than the fleet action was the single-ship combat, often between frigates, as in this print of the capture of the French 40-gunner Didon *by Capt. Thomas Baker of*

the 36-gun HMS Phoenix, *off Cape Finisterre on 10 August 1805: a typically ferocious, three-hour battle fought at never more than pistol range.*

A typical 'boat action': Lieut. Edward Nicholls RM and 13 seamen and marines from the frigate Blanche *capture a French cutter off San Domingo in November 1803, for which*

Nicholls received a sword from Lloyd's Patriotic Fund. The marines are clearly recognizable by their shoulder belts and 'round hats'.

or more) are even more remarkable: the French navy lost some 90 ships, whereas only one British ship of a similar nature was captured and not recovered.

Major 'fleet actions' were few, and after the virtual annihilation of a Franco-Spanish fleet at Trafalgar in 1805 opposing navies avoided the chance of a pitched battle, despite the fact that Napoleon endeavoured to construct a fleet capable of rivalling that of Britain. The great sea battles formed only a small part of the navy's duty, however; much of the most bitter fighting occurred in smaller actions, often between single ships, and in 'boat actions' and landings when the crews of Royal Navy vessels attacked French ships in harbour and shore installations. (Although it is difficult to classify some of the smaller actions, when the Naval General Service Medal was issued in 1848, of 231 authorized clasps, only some 17 (plus three for post-Napoleonic battles) were for what might be termed fleet actions; about 140 were awarded for single-ship or small squadron actions, about 60 for boat actions, and about 15 for shore actions.)

Napoleon's attempt to wreck British commerce by his 'Continental System'—which sought to deny Britain access to European ports—failed completely (British exports dropped only 7 per cent in 1807, and in the following year increased by 27 per cent). By contrast, the British naval blockade of French-

controlled ports virtually extinguished French overseas trade, so that by 1812–13 foreign commerce represented only 5.3 per cent of the total produce of Napoleon's empire.

Equally significant was the Royal Navy's offensive role, both in frustrating Napoleon's plans by the major naval battles (Aboukir Bay effectively decided the fate of the Egyptian campaign, and Copenhagen caused the collapse of the 'Armed Neutrality of the North'), and in supporting the army: no land campaign could have been undertaken or resupplied without the Royal Navy's uninterrupted control of the sea-lanes. In 1803, observing the agitation of a royal musician as a seaman carried his precious musical instrument, King George III remarked that there was no need for concern, as 'every thing is safe in the hands of a British seaman'; it was an appropriate comment upon the Royal Navy in general in the years of the 'Great War' against France.

Ships

Although this book concentrates upon the personnel of the Royal Navy, brief details of the ships are necessary. Excluding the smallest vessels—sloops, brigs, gunboats and hired coastal vessels—naval ships were classified or 'rated' according to the number of ports or 'perforations' through which a gun could be fired: thus a ship with its guns removed to act as a storeship or transport (said to be '*en flûte*') retained its original rating. The actual number of guns on a warship often exceeded the 'rating', as carronades (short-barrelled, large-bore guns used at close range) did not normally count towards a ship's rating; but exceptions included the 50-gunner *Glatton* which was armed experimentally with nothing but carronades. Ships of the line were the two- and three-decked 1st–4th rates, the 3rd rate 74-gunner being the most common; the 64- and especially 50-gunners were considerably weaker and not ideal for service in the line-of-battle. The smaller vessels included frigates (generally 32- to 44-gun 5th rates), 6th rates and sloops. Although there were variations, the accompanying Table A (from *The Bombardier and Pocket Gunner*, R.W. Adye, London 1802) is a reasonable guide.

Although most ships were built at home, many

Table A: Rating of Royal Navy Vessels, 1802

Rate	Gun-rating and actual ordnance	Carronades	Seamen
1st	100 (28 × 42pdr., 28 × 24pdr., 30 × 12pdr., 18 × 6pdr.)	2 × 32pdr., 6 × 24pdr.	875
2nd	98 (28 × 32pdr., 30 × 18pdr., 40 × 12pdr.)	2 × 32pdr., 6 × 18pdr.	750
3rd	80 (26 × 32pdr., 26 × 18pdr., 24 × 9pdr., 4 × 6 pdr.)	2 × 32pdr., 6 × 18pdr.	650
3rd	74 (28 × 32pdr., 28 × 18pdr. 18 × 9pdr.)	2 × 32pdr., 6 × 18pdr.,	650
3rd	70 (28 × 32pdr., 28 × 18pdr., 14 × 9pdr.)	2 × 32pdr., 6 × 18pdr.	650
3rd	64 (26 × 24pdr., 26 × 18pdr., 12 × 9pdr.)	2 × 24 pdr., 6 × 18pdr.	650
4th	50 (22 × 24pdr., 22 × 12pdr., 6 × 6pdr.)	6 × 24 pdr., 6 × 12pdr.	420
5th	44 (20 × 18pdr., 22 × 12pdr., 8 × 9pdr.)	8 × 18pdr.	300
5th	36 (26 × 18pdr., 2 × 12pdr., 8 × 9pdr.)	8 × 32pdr.	300
5th	32 (26 × 12pdr., 6 × 6pdr.)	6 × 24pdr.	300
6th	28 (24 × 9pdr., 4 × 6pdr.)	6 × 24pdr.	200
6th	24 (22 × 9pdr., 2 × 6pdr.)	2 × 24pdr., 6 × 18pdr.	200
6th	20 (20 × 9pdr.)	8 × 12pdr.	200
Sloop	18 (18 × 6pdr.)	8 × 12pdr.	125

(In practice, the 42-pdr. guns had been replaced by the more convenient 32-pdr.)
Marines were allocated to ships' companies at a rate of one per gun, plus: a captain and three subalterns for 74-gunners and above; a captain and two subalterns for a 64-gunner; two lieutenants for a 50-gunner; one subaltern for a 20 to 44-gunner; for a sloop, a sergeant was in command.

Table B: Royal Navy Dispositions, 1 July 1805

In commission	Ships of the line	44–50 gunners	Frigates	Sloops etc.
In port	14	5	21	80
English & Irish Channels	36	1	30	111
Downs & North Sea	8	7	13	132
West Indies and en route	17	–	19	29
Jamaica	2	–	10	25
America, Newfoundland	–	2	6	16
East Indies and en route	8	3	10	7
African coast	–	–	2	1
Spain, Portugal, Gibraltar	7	–	4	5
Mediterranean	1	–	13	12
Hospital and prison ships	15	1	1	–
Guard ships	3	2	4	–
Not in commission				
Receiving ships	6	4	7	1
Repairing	23	5	21	6
In ordinary (laid-up)	21	10	20	15
Building	16	–	15	27

A list of ships in commission in January 1806 provides details of the smaller vessels: 130 sloops (14–18 guns), 15 bomb-ketches (8 guns, 2 mortars), 1 fire-ship (14 guns), 101 gun-brigs (10–14 guns), 59 cutters (4–14 guns), and 52 troop- and store-ships; not including hired armed vessels for the protection of coastal trade.

(often superior) captured vessels were taken into service, often without a change of name: hence the use of foreign names like *Salvador del Mundo* (Spanish 112-gunner captured at St. Vincent); *Tre Kronen* and *Christian VII* (Danish 74 and 80 respectively, captured at Copenhagen in 1807); *Ca Ira* (French 80-gunner captured in 1795 and accidentally burned in 1796); *Rivoli* and *Marengo* (French 74 and 80 captured in 1812 and 1806 respectively). Ships might remain in service for generations: the 84-gunner *Royal William*, which served as a guardship from c.1790, was originally the 100-gunner *Prince* of 1670, rebuilt twice and renamed, and into its fifteenth decade of service when finally broken up in 1813.

Statistics published in 1803 exemplify the immense amount of material required for an 80-gunner: 1,600 tons of wood, 168 tons of guns, 51 tons of ammunition, 32 tons of cable, over 30 tons of rigging, 14 tons of sails, and 8 tons of paint and tar. Oak was

The national security provided by the Royal Navy's 'wooden walls' is epitomized by the design of this halfpenny token *issued by the Deptford ironmonger Thomas D. Haycraft, whose initials appear below the date '1795'.*

the principal hull timber, although teak used for ships built at Bombay and cedar used at Bermuda were good substitutes; but softwoods used experimentally because of shortages had no durability. In 1811 it was estimated that the construction of a 74-gunner would consume 50 acres of forest if the trees were planted 33 feet apart, and thus tree-planting was encouraged to ensure availability of timber for the future: between 1803 and 1809, for example, Lord Mansfield planted some 96,000 oaks at Scone, for which patriotic act he received the gold medal of the Society of Arts.

To illustrate the number of ships in commission at any one time, Table B shows the navy's disposition on 1 July 1805.

THE OFFICERS

The navy's entire administration was conducted by the Board of Admiralty, a staff of less than 60. The seven Lords Commissioners of the Admiralty were headed by the First Lord (usually a politician) and the First Professional Lord, a distinguished senior officer. Usually only one of these would be present to attend to routine business, and all but the most important orders (requiring the signatures of three board members) were issued by the Board Secretary, the chief civil servant. The administration was remarkably efficient, although the problem of communication gave admirals commanding overseas stations a degree of independence.

Before an officer could be commissioned he had to pass a seamanship examination, which could not be taken until the candidate had spent six years at sea, at least two in the rank of midshipman or master's mate. An aspirant officer could go to sea at a very early age as a 'volunteer' or captain's servant; and as a captain had total control over whom he took, such boys were usually the offspring of his relations or friends. Thus, 'patronage' was dominant from the very beginning, and continued through all levels, an admiral favouring or promoting his own followers or 'family' over those of another, although favours might be exchanged between admirals. Although this system had obvious potential for abuse, it worked surprisingly well, and the influence of such 'interest' was admitted openly. Thus, when Nelson's older brother Maurice died in 1801 while a secretary to the Navy Board his

Comparatively few of Nelson's 'wooden walls' survived to the era of photography. This is a somewhat unusual view of HMS Victory *firing her guns; the venerable first-rate 100-gunner was not dry-docked at Portsmouth until 1922.*

obituary noted that he 'was on the point of receiving, from the justice and liberality of ministers, an appointment suitable to his near consanguinity to the Hero of the Nile, and to his own individual merit'.

In a typical case, Basil Hall remarked that 'having no particular pretensions on aristocratic, or, indeed, on any other grounds, I saw no hope of advancement, except by getting on the list of some admiral on a foreign station'; in the event, he owed his commission to his father's support for Marquis Wellesley in Parliament, at a time when the Secretary of the Admiralty was William Wellesley Pole. Hall stated that the patronage system caused its beneficiaries to be doubly zealous in their conduct to justify their appointments, but it also caused worthy officers without influence to remain unemployed or unpromoted. For example, at his death in October 1807 Thomas Moody was at 93 one of the oldest lieutenants on the list; a protégé of Admiral Sir Charles Knowles, he had no further employment after that admiral retired in 1757. Charles Marshall, a lieutenant from 1759, held that rank for 45 years, 'with a most unblemished character for courage and professional skill', but retired after 'the daily mortification of seeing his juniors promoted over him'. John De la Touche, who died in October 1803 after 50 years' service, had been a lieutenant 28 years, 'but, his patrons quitting the Admiralty, he remained unemployed ever after'.

The reason for such unemployment was the fact that there were always many more officers than places for them; before the war less than a quarter were actually employed, and even with the wartime expansion of the service large numbers remained in retirement, drawing half-pay and officially liable for service, even though many were too old or infirm: in 1805 there were no fewer than 26 Royal Marine officers who had been drawing half-pay since the end of the Seven Years' War. Alternatively, an influential or successful officer could have a very full career: James Newman Newman (sic), lost as captain when the 74-gunner *Hero* was wrecked in the Texel in December 1811, was reported not to have spent more than six months on land in a period of 20 years. Even serious injury might not end a career: Charles Worsley Boys lost a leg at the 'Glorious First of June' at the age of 15, but served on and died in command of the 38-gunner *Statira* in November 1809.

Although many officers gained their first command experience as master's mate, many served as midshipmen, an intermediate appointment between commissioned and warrant officers. Although midshipmen were in effect trainee officers, the popular concept of them as young boys is not accurate: whils most ships would have a number of youths aboar aged 12–14, many as 'volunteers' gaining their 'sea time', many midshipmen were aged in their 20s an 30s, some in their 40s, and in one case a midshipma only passed his lieutenancy examination at the age of 57.

Officers progressed up the Navy list by seniority command of vessels being determined by rank normally a lieutenant was allowed to command onl an 'unrated' ship, a commander a 6th-rater, and captain a frigate or ship of the line. An office promoted to captain was said to have 'made post' (hence the term 'post-captain'), from where pro motion was by seniority through the three grade each of rear-admiral, vice-admiral and admiral Admirals were 'flag officers', i.e. those with a right t their own flag, the grades of each being described b the colours of the flags of the fleet's three squadrons from blue (the most junior), through white, to red – hence the ranks 'Rear Admiral of the Blue', 'Admira of the White', etc. The position of commodore intermediate between captain and rear-admiral, wa not a rank but a temporary appointment to permit a captain to command a squadron without having to attain the rank of admiral. In most cases promotion to flag rank was only attained after many years on half pay, and was not invariably automatic: Capt. John Fortescue, the oldest captain on the list (aged 87) a his death in May 1808, had not served at sea since 1763, and was one of 26 captains 'so irregularl'

The 1804 110-gun first-rate HMS Hibernia, which became base flagship at Malta in 1855 and was sold in 1902.

uperseded [sic] in their promotion to the rank of Admirals by Lord Howe', according to his obituary.

Unemployed officers did not always retire to home, however: for example, Capt. Charles Napier joined his cousins in the 52nd Foot in the Peninsula for a time as an 'amateur', 'not having a ship at that time and being too active and enterprising a fellow to remain at home idle waiting for one'. On the day before Busaco he joined the rearguard of the 14th Light Dragoons, 'fantastically dressed' in naval uniform, with a cutlass and brace of pistols at his waist and riding a conspicuous white pony; and so annoyed the 14th's Capt. Brotherton by urging him to charge everything in sight, that Brotherton was quite relieved when Napier was slightly wounded in the leg and went to the rear. He was back with the 52nd for the Battle of Busaco. Equally adventurous was Capt. Nesbit Willoughby, who served as a Russian colonel in the 1812 campaign while on half-pay, 'a man who thrust his head into every gun, and ran it against every stone wall, he could find from Cape Cormorin to Moscow … his face was cut and hacked in all directions', according to Blakiston of the Portuguese service.

THE LOWER DECKS

The Royal Navy's demand for seamen was insatiable, its authorised strength rising from 45,000 at the outbreak of war to 145,000 in 1810–13; although less than 1,900 men were killed in the major actions, over 85,000 died of disease, accident or shipwreck, and large numbers were invalided. To fill the ranks, volunteers were preferred and encouraged by a cash bounty; and from 1795 the Quota Act compelled every county to provide a number of recruits according to its population (or be fined), so that civic authorities offered bounties or remitted the sentences of malefactors on condition they enlisted. Even so, forcible impressment was also necessary.

The 'press gang' originated in the 13th century,

The press gang 'recruits' a landsman: a contemporary print which shows a lieutenant armed with a cudgel, wearing a shoulder belt with oval plate; the seamen are shown with 'round hats' and either striped trousers or 'petticoat breeches'.

The remains of the 36-gun frigate Belvidera, built 1809, and in harbour service from 1846 until sold in 1906.

and involved the forcible abduction of men and their conscription into the navy irrespective of circumstances, providing that they were aged between 18 and 55 and were not apprentices, though these exemptions were not always observed. Trained merchant seamen were the preferred targets (merchant ships were often stopped en route to port and likely recruits taken off), but press-gangs also ranged ashore to conscript 'landsmen'.

The Impress Service was naturally unpopular: in 1798 *The Morning Chronicle* claimed that impressment was so absurd a method of recruitment that even Swift in *Gulliver's Travels*, 'though he drew occasionally upon his imagination to heighten or multiply follies, he could not stretch so far as this'. Impressment was often resisted; for example, in June 1795 during a 'hot press' on the Thames, a press-gang was forcibly evicted from a Liverpool trader, a 'desperate affray' in which one of the gang was reported killed. In 1803 the boats of three naval vessels, attempting to board two East Indiamen in the Thames, were repelled by pikes, cutlasses and thrown roundshot, an affair ending in the death of two merchant seamen when the officer in command of the press-gang ordered his men to fire. Some civic authorities restricted the actions of the Impress Service: in May 1798, for example, the Lord Mayor of London ordered that pressing should only take place after 10 p.m., and be restricted to disorderly persons and those 'who cannot give a satisfactory account of themselves'. Yet the service remained so unpopular that in December 1811 a near-riot freed a suspected murderer from police custody, the mob mistakenly believing that he was being pressed!

It is impossible to determine the exact proportion of pressed men, as those abducted from merchant ships at sea might choose to volunteer and receive a bounty since they had no escape, but the system did work; and as each ship's crew was discharged at the end of its commission, the conscription was for only a limited period.

Foreigners made up a considerable proportion of the navy: over ten per cent of the crew of HMS *Victory* at Trafalgar, for example, was non-British, including among at least 15 nationalities many Americans, Frenchmen, West Indians, and even a Russian. Ships operating in the Caribbean or East Indies probably had a larger number of recruits from The number of Americans in the Royal Navy was considerable: it was stated in Parliament in 1813 that 6,600 Americans had obtained their discharges from the navy in 1811–12. Although impressment was one of the American complaints which led to the War of 1812, Americans were officially immune from 'pressing' upon the production of a 'protection', a document certifying American birth. Many of these were given by American officials to British seamen who masqueraded as Americans to avoid impressment, much to British indignation: an article in *The Gentleman's Magazine* in 1812 stated that those who sought false 'protections' were only 'wretches who, remaining in our service, would but disgrace it; still the fact is damning evidence of American depravity . . . insolence and falsehood'.

Promotion from the 'lower decks' (where the seamen lived) went from 'landsman' (i.e. an untrained seaman) to ordinary and able seaman, to those possessing special skills such as sailmaker or carpenter (termed 'idlers' because their specialist duties precluded them from standing watch). The 'petty officers' (boatswains and mates, etc.) were appointed by the captain, but the higher ranks were appointed by a warrant issued by one of the Admiralty's specialist departments, hence the term 'Warrant Officer'. The senior ones enjoyed 'wardroom rank', i.e. the status of officers; but their assistants, classed

The press gang at work by the Tower of London. This engraving by Barrow after Collings shows the members of the gang armed with cudgels; the lieutenant (right centre), wearing a black shoulder belt, appears to be rewarding an innkeeper who has assisted the gang in making its captures.

Admiral Richard Kempenfelt (1735–86): exemplifying the lax interpretation of dress regulations, this engraving by H. Robinson after Tilly Kettle shows a very plain service or undress uniform for which there appears to have been no authorization. The 'fighting sword' is a plain, curved hanger.

Alexander Hood, Lord Bridport (brother of Samuel, Lord Hood) wearing undress uniform of an admiral, 1787–95; note the number of loops on the lapels. The breast star is that of the Order of the Bath, and the chain that of the large Naval Gold Medal for the Glorious First of June, only six of which were awarded with a gold chain. (Engraving by S. Freeman after Lemuel Abbott)

as 'master's mates', and the ship's gunner, carpenter, etc., did not. The senior Warrant Officer was the Master (originally 'sailing master'), an experienced seaman appointed by the Navy Board and responsible for all matters of navigation. The importance of this appointment and of the Master's relationship with his commanding officer may be exemplified by an exchange between Lord Howe and the Master of HMS *Queen Charlotte* at the 'Glorious First of June', James Bowen: the Master queried an order, fearing that it would cause a collision with a French ship, to which Howe brusquely repeated the order. Bowen muttered loud enough for all to hear, 'Damned if I care, if you don't. I'll take you near enough to singe your black whiskers!'

Surgeons were Warrant Officers appointed by the Sick and Hurt Office, present on all major vessels, to treat both wounds and illness. Some stations, and indeed ships, were renowned as being 'sickly', though the reasons given were sometimes unscientific: the bad health record of one frigate was explained by its transportation of French prisoners, whose 'foreign nastinesses and abominations' had so impregnated the ship that even repeated fumigations 'could not eradicate the unhealthy taint'!

Pursers were Warrant Officers appointed by the Victualling Office, personally financially responsible for all food and clothing on their ship. They were poorly paid, but were permitted to make a profit of $12\frac{1}{2}$ per cent on all except tobacco (10 per cent) and 'slops' (5 per cent); and made an additional profit by issuing food in pounds of 14 ozs. (butter in 'pounds' of 12 ozs. and cheese 9 ozs.). (One of the grievances which caused the Spithead and Nore mutinies was this supply of short measures, the mutineers demanding that rations should be issued in 16-oz.

Thomas, a major landowner and 'eminent attorney' was convicted of attempting to defraud the Navy Board over supply of timber.

Although mentioned infrequently in contemporary sources, many ships maintained a band of music apart from those who performed for recreation and to accompany the routine shipboard tasks ('a fifer or a fiddler usually plays some of their favourite tunes and it is quite delightful to see the glee with which Jack will "stamp and go", keeping exact time to "Jack's the lad" or the "College Hornpipe"', during 'the performance of the various evolutions', as 'R.B.' recalled in the *United Service Journal* in 1834). A ship's band might play to hearten the crew when going into action, and some maintained bands as large as those of an army regiment: for example, the 74-gunner *San Domingo* had 15 in her band in 1812, the 120-gunner *Caledonia* ten in 1811. Bands were not restricted to the larger vessels: the 32-gun frigate *Jason* had a band in 1814, for example; and when the 50-gunner *Endymion* supplied equipment to Spanish guerrillas during the Peninsular War, 'one of our most showy drums, brought from this ship, was bestowed upon the army, to their unspeakable delight', according to Basil Hall. Even professional

Richard, Earl Howe (1726–99): 'Black Dick' in the 1795 dress uniform of an admiral, showing the cuff loops extending over the three rank laces. (Engraving by W. T. Fry after Gainsborough Dupont)

pounds as on shore.) The practice was permitted officially to offset frauds perpetrated by the provision-suppliers, who frequently sold the navy food in short measure or which was many years old; and without such additional opportunities for profit fewer pursers could have been found, as each had to deposit a substantial sum as a 'bond' with the Navy Board.

Frauds were common in all types of supply; an enquiry in 1803 uncovered phenomenal dishonesty, such as a cooperage contract which cost 27 times the material's value; and the frauds could be perpetrated by unlikely sources. For example, in 1800 one George

Adam, Viscount Duncan of Camperdown (1731–1804), in 1795 dress uniform. Note the unusually large number of lapel loops (apparently 12) and the three cuff rings of admiral's rank; the sword is apparently that awarded by the City of London for Camperdown. The Naval Gold Medal is that for Camperdown, the breast star and ribbon those of the Russian Order of Alexander Nevski (awarded 1797); in Smart's portrait drawing of 1798 the ribbon is worn under the coat. (Engraving after John Hoppner)

musicians were employed: when the composer Moorhead was forced by penury to enlist in 1803, he was given mastership of the band of the 74-gunner *Monarch* by her Captain Serle, but despite this favoured position the change in his circumstances so dispirited him that he hanged himself in April 1804.

Although women flocked aboard ships in port, an indulgence permitted officially, none were supposed to go to sea; but women were often carried aboard ship, generally wives of petty officers. In action they might assist the surgeon, and were sufficiently numerous for some to be refused the Navy General Service Medal on the grounds that the award of any would cause a flood of applications. (One application was made by Daniel Tremendous McKenzie, who was born upon HMS *Tremendous* during the battle of the 'Glorious First of June', the clasp for which he applied!) Occasionally women masqueraded as seamen: in 1815 *The Times* reported that a 'rather handsome' African woman had served aboard *Queen Charlotte* under the name of Able Seaman William Brown, having enlisted following a quarrel with her husband, and becoming a most efficient member of the crew. Women sailed in the smallest vessels: when the 18-gun brig *Pandora* was wrecked in the Cattegat in February 1811, nine women were among the 109 persons saved.

The popular concept of brutal floggings with a cat-o'-nine-tails is often exaggerated, for although the enforcement of discipline was necessarily strict, given the calibre of some of the recruits, the system worked reasonably well. Bound by the 36 Articles of War, enforceable by court-martial and death penalty, at sea a captain was in total command; but excluding the occasional lunatic or sadist, cases of officers exceeding reasonable force were few, such transgressors being liable for severe punishment. (In 1812 Lieut. Gamage of the sloop *Griffon* was hanged aboard his own ship for killing a marine sergeant who had disobeyed orders with insolence.) It is notable that the severity of discipline was not one of the seamen's complaints during the 'great mutiny'.

The most famous case of tyranny was probably that of Capt. Pigot of the frigate *Hermione*, whose behaviour was so obnoxious that he was murdered by his crew, who handed the ship to Spain. In a celebrated exploit it was recovered in a raid by Sir Edward Hamilton, yet despite his resulting fame he

George Henry Towry (1767–1809) commanded the 64-gun Diadem *at St. Vincent, but after his health broke down on an arduous winter cruise in the Channel aboard the frigate* Tribune *he retired and was appointed to the Transport Board. This engraving by Ridley after Jean shows a very early pattern of captain's epaulette, virtually a fringed shoulder strap.*

was himself court-martialled and dismissed for using unreasonable force, in tying men to the rigging. Some verdicts on officers' behaviour appear odd, however: the lieutenant of the hired armed ship *Humber*, who in May 1806 shot dead a would-be deserter, escaped punishment when the coroner's jury returned a verdict of accidental death! In a few cases, grudges against officers turned into something worse; for example, in December 1808 Capt. Balderston of the 10-gun sloop *Parthian* was killed by a pistol-shot in the back, fired by Master's Mate Smith, on deck and in the presence of the purser; Smith, a man 'addicted to drinking', was hanged. Less severe retribution was administered by Rev. William Holmes, who had been dismissed as chaplain of his ship for criticizing the captain; on next meeting his late commander in the streets of Yarmouth, the clergyman administered a public caning!

Although desertion was always a problem, in

general discipline was maintained well and was a crucial factor in the good performance of duty. Indeed, when aboard HMS *Bellerophon* in 1815 Napoleon remarked upon the quiet, competent and disciplined manner in which all duties were performed: 'What I admire most in your ship is the extreme silence and orderly conduct of your men. On board a French ship every one calls and gives orders; and they gabble like so many geese.'

AUXILIARIES

Even merchant ships might engage in combat just as bitter as that which involved the navy. For example, in January 1811 the merchantman *Cumberland* fought off the attack of four French privateers in the English Channel, and four boardings, by the somewhat unusual expedient of withdrawing all the 26-man crew into the cabin, allowing the French to come aboard, and then charging out en masse to clear the deck. One of the *Cumberland*'s crew was killed and the chief mate wounded, but losses among the 270 Frenchmen were reported as 60. So impressed was the Admiralty by this heroic defence that each of *Cumberland*'s crew was given three years' exemption from impressment.

The transportation of supplies and the military was the responsibility of the **Transport Board**, formed 1794, whose six commissioners and agents in major ports were Royal Navy captains and lieutenants who arranged for the hire of merchant vessels and crews; some hired-in ships, classed as 'armed transports', had naval crews.

The revenue service was divided between the **Boards of Customs and Boards of Excise** of England and Scotland, and a combined Board for Ireland. Responsible for the suppression of smuggling and the collection of dues levied on certain goods, much of their operation was land-based, but the Boards maintained small flotillas of revenue vessels capable of engaging lightly armed privateers and of supporting the navy; some were deployed in support of the Walcheren expedition, for example. In 1809 the service was reorganized as the 'Preventative Water Guard'. The maritime revenue officers wore a uniform like that of the Royal Navy, without epaulettes; in 1804 they were refused permission to wear silver epaulettes lest they be mistaken for real naval officers.

The **Packet Service**, maintained by the Post Office, comprised a number of small, fast vessels, the largest operating the transatlantic routes. They fulfilled a vital communications role, and were involved in numerous fights and chases, perhaps most notably that off Cuba in November 1798, when the packet *Antelope* fought off a French privateer. Aided by French civilian passengers and a French royalist ex-naval officer, and despite being outnumbered three to one, the crew killed two-thirds of the privateers and took their ship as a prize to Jamaica. A portrait of a packet commander shows a uniform similar to that of the Royal Navy, including a laced hat, blue coat with standing collar worn closed and with 'triangles' turned back at the neck, with short gold loops on the turned-back lapels and on the right-hand row of breast-buttons, and one loop on the collar.

The **East India Company** maintained a small force of sloops, schooners and brigs, based at Bombay and intended to protect East India traders. On occasion they assisted the Royal Navy in East Indian waters; and some of their personnel offered their services during the Spithead and Nore mutinies, one of their officers, Charles Handley, being especially

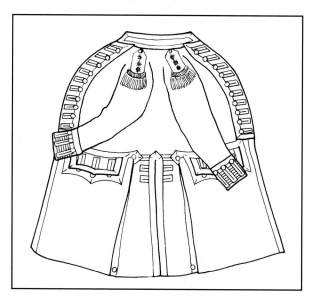

The pattern of dress coat according to the 1795 regulations; this example, with the cuff- and epaulette-insignia of an admiral, has ten lapel loops and shows the design of lace on the pockets and rear skirts.

commended for commanding a gun-boat at this period.

The **Sea Fencible** service was formed in May 1798 as a maritime 'home guard' based on coastal towns (but including the London River Fencibles), trained to man shore batteries and light vessels for coastal patrol. Their part-time service equated to that of the military Volunteer Force, their exemption from impressment and the militia ballot being a greater incentive to join than the pay for days spent on service; their commanders were naval officers. Although the Sea Fencibles would probably have been useful in the event of invasion they attracted much criticism (St. Vincent remarked that their main function was to calm the fears of old ladies, both inside and outside the Admiralty!), and they were disbanded in 1810.

Other 'auxiliaries' included the privateers— small, privately owned warships operating against the enemy by the authority of an Admiralty 'letter of marque', without which their actions would have been piracy. Under the pressures of war, all manner of unsavoury characters were employed: for example, in the 1799 expedition to the Netherlands the notorious smuggler and prison-breaker Johnson was used as a guide to the Dutch coast, in return for a pardon. He soon returned to his old habits, and in 1802 staged a daring escape from Fleet prison.

UNIFORMS

Officers

Not until 1748 was an attempt made to establish a uniform dress for officers of the Royal Navy, any previous uniformity being almost accidental and generally restricted to the followers of individual officers (such as the grey coats with red facings and silver lace worn by Capt. Wyndham and his officers of the 70-gunner *Kent* in 1743). Otherwise officers wore clothing according to their own taste, generally red or blue and cut in the current civilian style. Blue coats with white facings and gold lace was chosen as the first uniform, perhaps inspired by a coat designed by Capt. Philip Saumarez (killed 1747), or (perhaps apocryphally) after the King had seen the Duchess of Bedford in a striking riding habit in these colours. Save for the adoption of scarlet facings in 1830–43,

Alan, Baron Gardner (1742–1809), in the 1795 uniform of a vice-admiral, showing two stars on the epaulettes and the lapels hooked together. The medal and chain is presumably that awarded for the 'Glorious First of June'. (Engraving by Fenner after Sir William Beechey)

this colour scheme remained the naval regulation thereafter.

The elaborately laced dress coat worn by flag officers, with a plainer 'frock' uniform for undress, was replaced in 1767 by a laced but less ornate coat for all purposes, which appears to have prompted the use of plainer undress coats by some flag officers, for which no regulation appears to have existed. In 1774 captains and commanders were ordered to convert their universal coats into full dress by the addition of more lace, and to wear plain 'frocks' for undress; waistcoats, which had been white from the earliest period, were no longer to carry lace, and white breeches replaced the previous blue. Full dress was restored to flag officers in 1783.

The 1787 uniform

Throughout the period, the cut and style of officers' uniform resembled that of the army, itself based upon the prevailing civilian style, with a number of variations such as the practice of not folding back the coat-skirts to create turnbacks. The uniform regulated in October 1787 again reduced the decoration upon flag officers' uniform. The full dress coat or 'frock' for flag officers was blue cloth, with gold lace edging the front opening (no lapels) and blue standing collar, edging the horizontal pockets and flaps, with bands of lace encircling the white cuff— one band for rear-admirals, two for vice-admirals, and three for admirals. On each side of the breast were pointed gold lace loops, equally spaced for an admiral, in pairs for a rear-admiral and in threes for a vice-admiral; nine or ten appears to have been the usual number. The flat gilt buttons bore a fouled anchor device, with a half spray of laurel around the base and on one side of the anchor: one button to each breast-loop, and three on each cuff and pocket flap. No epaulettes were worn by any officers at this period. The coat lining was specified originally as white silk, changed to simply 'white' some six weeks after the original order.

With this coat were worn the usual white shirt, single-breasted white waistcoat with small gilt buttons (including three per pocket flap), white breeches and stockings, and buckled shoes. The hat retained a trace of the original tricorn shape but by this period was virtually a bicorn, worn 'athwart', with broad gold lace edging, a black cockade at the left front secured by a gold loop and gilt button, and a mixed gold and blue cord around the crown with tasselled ends, often visible at the corners of the hat.

For ordinary dress flag officers had a plain 'frock' (a term being replaced by 'undress'), a double-breasted coat blue throughout, save for a white lining, with a standing collar and plain cuffs, and lapels which could be worn folded back, to reveal pointed gold loops arranged as on the dress coat, or fastened over to conceal the loops; the tops of the lapels might be turned back to form 'triangles' at the neck. The three buttons on each cuff and pocket flap had gold loops, and an additional loop and button was carried on each side of the collar; buttons were as for the dress coat. The same smallclothes were worn as in full dress; as there were no regulations covering headdress, whilst it was possible to wear an unlaced hat with undress uniform, laced hats were also worn. The lace used at this period for officers' uniforms appears to have been woven with a diagonal or 'crooked bias' pattern; before 1787 and after 1795 it was 'vellum', of interwoven longitudinal design.

Captains' full dress is described in the commentary to our Plate A2, and the undress coat in that for Plate B2. For both the buttons were flat, gilt, with a roped edge and bearing a fouled anchor upon a reeded ground, within a roped oval. Smallclothes where white and hats like those of flag officers, laced and unlaced versions apparently being worn indiscriminately. Commodores with captains under their command, the First Captain to the Admiral of the Fleet, and First Captains to admirals commanding squadrons of 20 ships of the line, were permitted to wear the uniform of a rear-admiral.

The next rank down from captain was that of commander (officially 'master and commander' until

Nelson in full dress, with symbols of his victories: the chelengk *on his hat recalling Aboukir Bay, and a captured Spanish flag and sword representing St. Vincent. He presented the sword of a Spanish admiral to the corporation of Norwich (for which this picture was painted), Nelson having received the freedom of that city. (Engraving by Edward Bell after Sir William Beechey, painted 1800–01)*

Nelson in undress uniform, with rank insignia of a Rear-Admiral (note the single epaulette-star). The coat is presumably the undress uniform of a captain, to which flag officer's rank distinctions have been added (flag officers' undress coats had standing collars), and is also shown in a portrait by Henry Edridge. The coat is apparently that worn when his arm was lost: tears are visible in the right upper sleeve. The star is that of the Order of the Bath, the Gold Medal that for St. Vincent. (Engraving by R. Graves after Lemuel Abbott)

Nelson in undress uniform, wearing the chelengk on his hat, and the ribbon of the Order of the Bath over the right shoulder. Another version of the same painting shows the St. Vincent Gold Medal around the neck in addition to the medallions and breast-stars shown here. (Engraving by T.W. Harland after Lemuel Abbott)

1794), whose dress uniform was like that of a junior captain, but with blue lapels and cuffs instead of white; their undress coat was like that of captains, but with ten loops on the breast, in pairs. The 1787 regulations restored full and undress uniform to lieutenants, in place of a single uniform worn from 1767; for their dress uniform, see the commentary to Plate A3, and for undress that to Plate B3.

The 1795 uniform

Changes in uniform for all ranks above lieutenant were announced by the Admiralty on 1 June 1795, and repeated later in the month (e.g. in the *London Chronicle* on 6 June), although officers were allowed to wear their existing uniform until 1 June 1796. For all ranks the lace was to be that used before 1787, wider for flag officers, and white facings were discontinued for all ranks above lieutenant.

For flag officers, the dress coat was blue with a blue standing collar, blue lapels and round cuffs; collar and lapels were edged with broad gold lace, with double gold lace on the horizontal pockets and upper edge of the cuffs. (Collar-lace was not mentioned in the regulations; a portrait by Henry Bone of Capt. J.W. Payne, who commanded HMS *Russell* at the First of June, shows such wide collar-lace that only a narrow strip of blue collar is visible). Gold loops were ordered for the button-holes, and although the design was not specified they were generally square-ended and borne upon the lapels (9), cuffs (3), and pockets; a portrait of Lord Barham, however, shows pointed loops.

For the first time, epaulettes were introduced

officially (though evidence exists for unofficial use as early as 1783), of gold lace with bullion fringe, worn on both shoulders. Flag officers' rank was distinguished by epaulette-badges and lace rings on the cuff: admirals, three silver epaulette-stars, three gold rings; vice-admirals, two stars, two rings; and rear-admirals, one. The epaulette-stars had eight points. In some cases the cuff-rings appear little different from the upper cuff-edging, but were sometimes much narrower, e.g. as shown in Slater's 1813 portrait of Gambier. Coat-lining, waistcoat and breeches remained white, and a gold-laced hat was specified. The undress uniform was described as a plain blue coat with lapels, standing collar and the buttons 'now in use', devoid of lace except for gold rank-rings on the cuff, and epaulettes, as for full dress. Minor variations existed: one of Nelson's coats has a small button and hole on each side of the collar, and Jean's 1801 portrait of James De Saumarez as a rear-admiral appears to show only eight buttons per lapel (as does a portrait of Capt. Henry Blackwood). Abbott's 1795 portrait of Jervis shows the epaulette-button mid-way up the collar; and in his portrait of Capt. John Cooke (captain of HMS *Bellerophon*, killed at Trafalgar), the epaulette-button is on the lower collar-lace.

For captains, the white facings were changed to blue, and the 'long slash sleeve, as formerly worn' was restored to full dress, having been discontinued in 1787; this 'slash' was a three-pointed flap bearing three buttons. The lapels and standing collar had a single line of gold lace edging, but the cuffs and pockets a double line; the lapels had blue thread loops, which appear quite prominently in some portraits, such as that of the hydrographer Matthew Flinders. Two plain gold epaulettes were to be worn by captains of 'three years' post', and a single epaulette on the right shoulder by more junior captains. Lining, waistcoat and breeches remained white, and gold-laced hats were specified for full dress. The undress coat was plain blue, with lapels, with buttons on lapels, cuffs and pockets, but devoid of lace. Epaulettes were as for the dress coat, but made so as to 'take off and put on occasionally', secured by lace or cloth loops at the point of the shoulder, although the occasions when they should be omitted were not stated. Although not specified in the regulations, contemporary illustrations and tailors' patterns show the collar of the undress coat to have been of the stand-and-fall variety, at least in the majority of cases; and apparently the coat-lining was dark blue, although both Eckstein's and Ker Porter's portraits of Sir Sidney Smith at Acre show white lining. The regulations specified that an unlaced hat should be worn with the undress coat, and 'blue breeches, as may be convenient'.

For commanders, the new uniform was like that of captains, but with an epaulette on the left shoulder only. The full dress cuff-lace seems generally to have had a double row on the flap but a single row around the upper edge of the cuff, but although this may have become a differentiation of rank from that of captain it had no official recognition.

The adoption of epaulettes may have been prompted by the need to identify the wearers as commissioned officers, especially when encountering nations to whom an epaulette was an acknowledged

Nelson in full dress; this engraving by H. Robinson is one of several taken from Hoppner's portrait of 1800, which shows white breeches, stockings, and buckled shoes. Note how one star overlaps the turned-back lapel. (The copy of the Guzzardi portrait presented to the Sultan shows the Order of the Crescent on the right breast, but this was almost certainly done to flatter the Sultan by showing his decoration more prominently.)

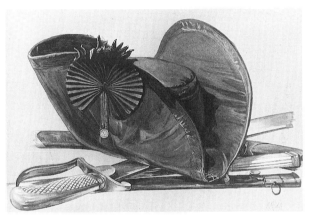

Nelson's cocked hat (with gold binding and loop) which was placed upon his coffin in the funeral procession. The sword was that carried at St. Vincent (gilt hilt and chequered ivory grip); his dirk had a reeded grip and gilt cushion-shaped pommel and quillons. (Print after W. Gibb)

Nelson in the uniform worn at Trafalgar, from sketches made by Dr. Beatty during the autopsy; note the plain hat with black silk cockade loop and green eye shade, worn with vice-admiral's undress uniform. (Engraving by E. Scriven)

symbol of rank; but their adoption was not universally popular, epaulettes being regarded as a French ornament. Probably before the full implementation of the 1795 regulation uniform, epaulettes were added to the 1787 uniform; Horatio Nelson, for example, purchased his first epaulettes in Genoa in mid-July 1795, remarkably soon after the publication of the regulation, presumably adding them to his existing coats. He noted that in order to ensure the acquisition of an acceptable pair he took a military officer with him to advise—perhaps Charles Pierson of the 69th Foot, then serving as marines aboard Nelson's *Agamemnon*—which suggests that there may have been considerable differences of design among the early epaulettes.

The cut of the coat altered slightly during the period, the skirts becoming more sharply angled from the waist and the lapels shorter; it became fashionable to wear the lapels buttoned across, sometimes only partially, with upper and lower buttons unfastened and the lapels partially turned back. The single-breasted waistcoat with 'skirts' remained correct for full dress, but shorter patterns, sometimes double-breasted, became fashionable for both dress and undress.

In addition to the blue breeches permitted for undress, blue or white pantaloons became popular by the end of the 18th century (although not recognized officially until 1825), worn with either military-style Hessian or half boots. A plate of a lieutenant's uniform published in *The Naval Magazine* in 1800, showing blue pantaloons and apparently soft, calf-length half boots, is described as depicting the uniform worn on all except 'the most particular occasions of ceremony'. Loose trousers became increasingly popular for service wear, but were not accepted officially for formal occasions: a lieutenant who reported for orders to the Admiralty in 1815 wearing a dress coat and white trousers was told to come back when he was more presentable! Breeches, stockings and shoes remained the formal dress, and indeed an officer of HMS *Victory* recalled that he only ever saw Nelson wear boots on two occasions, and then only briefly and in wet weather. Some advocated the use of stockings in action as being more manageable for the surgeon in case of injury.

Such was the level of violation of regulations that St. Vincent issued a strong rebuke in 1797 against officers appearing on shore dressed like shopkeepers in 'coloured' clothes (i.e. civilian dress), or in uniform

Sir Thomas Troubridge Bt. in the dress uniform of a rear-admiral, wearing the Nile and St. Vincent Gold Medals and the Order of St. Ferdinand and Merit. W. Holl's engraving accurately reproduces Sir William Beechey's original, painted 1804–06, including the unfastened upper lapel-buttons, and the cuff variation in which the rank-lace passes over the loops. (Similar arrangement of lace is shown in Slater's portraits of Gambier and Duckworth, for example.) Troubridge was lost when HMS Blenheim was wrecked on Rodriguez Island in the Indian Ocean in February 1807.

with 'round hats'—a style popular in the 1790s but permitted to be worn only at sea, and sanctioned officially only in 1825.

The bicorn with pronounced front 'peak' gave way by the turn of the century to a flatter bicorn, usually worn 'fore-and-aft' by officers below flag rank, admirals generally retaining the 'athwart' style, although this was not covered by regulations; a portrait of Thomas Hardy shows an intermediate style, with the right corner advanced. Very large hat-tassels are shown in some illustrations, for example Edridge's 1807 portrait of Sir Thomas Foley. An unusual hat-ornament features in many portraits of Nelson, a 13-rayed diamond jewel or *chelengk* presented by the Sultan of Turkey (with the Order of the Crescent and a scarlet-lined sable pelisse) in recognition of his victory of Aboukir Bay; each ray represented a French ship destroyed, and the jewelled centre included a star which revolved by clockwork! Nelson appears to have worn this on a laced hat with both dress and undress uniform; although the well-known portrait by Leonardo Guzzardi, painted in Palermo in 1799, which shows the hat pushed well back on the head, represents neither a new fashion nor an attempt to balance the jewel, but simply a style to keep the edge of the hat away from the wound over the right eye sustained in the battle of Aboukir Bay. A similar jewelled ornament and pelisse were presented to Sir Sidney Smith for leading the defence of Acre in 1799.

Black stocks and a white shirt-frill were the usual neck-wear throughout the period, although white neckcloths were also used (for example in Lawrence's portrait of Graham Moore, apparently as a commander c.1791, worn with a loose white bow-tie); in Opie's portrait of Sidney Smith, painted c.1783, the shirt-frill is affixed by what appears to be a pin in the design of the Union flag. Greatcoats, necessary for wear on deck in bad weather, would have been possessed almost universally, but were not regulated and would have been of civilian patterns.

A new commissioned rank was introduced in 1804, that of sub-lieutenant; these officers wore the undress uniform of lieutenants at all times, and possessed no dress version. An unusual variation on the standard uniform was worn by the officers attending Nelson's funeral: not only with the usual black crape around the arms and hats, but black waistcoats, breeches and stockings as well.

The 1812 uniform

Amendments made in March 1812 to officers' uniform affected principally full dress, for which white facings were restored; for details, see the commentary to Plate L.

Warrant officers

Uniforms for warrant officers were first regulated in November 1787. All wore a blue coat with blue lapels, round cuffs and falling collar, three buttons on each cuff and pocket and generally nine on each lapel; white lining, waistcoat and breeches; presumably a plain hat (not mentioned in the regulations); buttons were gilt, bearing a fouled anchor. Masters' mates had a blue coat with white 'edging', no lapels, blue falling collar, blue round cuffs with three buttons, and three buttons on the pocket; white lining, waistcoat and breeches; and buttons like those of warrant officers.

In 1805 medical officers were given parity with army surgeons, and consequently a distinctive uniform, as detailed below. The other warrant officers (masters and pursers) were authorized a dress uniform in August 1807, as before but with a standing collar (with button and hole on each side), and new buttons. For masters these bore the insignia of the Navy Board, two small anchors at the sides of a large anchor, upon a reeded ground within a roped oval, with roped edge; pursers' buttons bore the insignia of the Victualling Office, crossed fouled anchors upon a reeded ground within a roped oval, with a roped edge. The old uniform, with new buttons, was used henceforth for undress, with blue or white breeches. The use of the old coat with old buttons was extended to lower-ranking personnel, gunners, carpenters and boatswains, and masters' mates' uniforms were amended by the addition of standing collars with button and hole. An unofficial badge of office was the 'boatswain's call' or whistle, often worn on a chain or cord around the neck, some being of the finest quality of silversmithing.

In 1812 all the above buttons were altered by the addition of a crown over the device. An additional button, not mentioned before, was that worn by officers of the transport service, bearing the insignia of the Transport Office—a crossed anchor and cannon barrel.

Medical officers

The two grades of medical officer were those of physician and surgeon, the former a more exalted position and consequently with a more ornate uniform. To differentiate them from ordinary ships' surgeons, it appears that personally designed uniforms were not unknown: one recorded example included a blue coat with blue lapels, falling collar and cuffs, all laced gold. Naval physicians had petitioned to be permitted to wear epaulettes, which was refused, and the original suggestion that medical officers should have black velvet facings was also rejected; but in June 1805 medical officers' uniform

Cuthbert Collingwood (1750–1810) in the 1795 regulation dress uniform of a vice-admiral. The epaulette bears the correct two stars of rank, but the two rings of cuff lace are apparently taken to include the cuff edging, instead of the edge plus two rank rings. The rank-lace passes over the cuff loops. Note also the enamelled 'presentation' smallsword. (Mezzotint by Charles Turner after the portrait painted from life by Giuseppi Politi of Syracuse in December 1807)

was regulated. Thereafter, physicians wore a blue full dress coat with standing collar, two rows of half-inch gold lace on the collar and cuffs, three buttons on the cuff and pocket; white lining, waistcoat and breeches; and unlaced hat. Devis' portrait of Dr. Beatty as a physician shows the collar lace set so as to reveal a blue line between the two rows. For undress, the coat had a falling collar, no lace, but three buttons on the cuff and pocket; blue or white waistcoat and breeches according to personal taste; and the same hat. For surgeons, see Plate J2. Buttons of those serving aboard ship bore an anchor within a roped oval, and those ashore the same with the letters 'HS' ('hospital staff') on either side of the anchor; use was also made of the insignia of the Sick and Hurt Office, a fouled anchor within a roped oval, with a roped edge. Assistant surgeons, hospital mates and dispensers

James, Baron Gambier
(1756–1833), showing flag
officers' dress uniform
with lapels hooked
together, and the Gold
Medal for St. Vincent. A
religious man, Gambier
was known in the navy as
'Dismal Jimmy'.
(Engraving by W. Holl
after a portrait by
Beechey, painted probably
in 1808)

The collar patch, styled a 'turnback' in the regulations (originally being part of the collar turned back to reveal the white lining), bore a single button and embroidered blue loop. A bicorn, unlaced except for the universal cockade loop, was the usual headdress, although 'round hats' are recorded as an alternative as early as 1780. There were no official alterations in midshipmen's uniform during the period, although contemporary pictures show a progressive change in style as with officers' coats, and the use of trousers instead of breeches and stockings, and of 'round hats', was widespread: see Plate K3. More elaborate costumes included those worn by the midshipmen of the 50-gunner *Antelope* at the end of the period under review, including tight white pantaloons, Hessian boots with gold twisted cord edging and bullion tassels, and bicorns. For undress, see Plate K4.

Officers' swords

A sword formed part of the equipment of all officers and warrant officers, but was not always carried at sea except when action was imminent (Surgeon Beatty recorded that for the first time in action, Nelson forgot to wear his sword at Trafalgar; having been

had only one uniform, similar to those of the higher appointments but only those of dispensers with lapels; and blue or white smallclothes according to individual choice. From June 1805 physicians and surgeons were permitted to carry the regulation officer's sword.

Midshipmen

The 1787 regulations confirmed the uniform of midshipmen which appears to have been worn for some time before that date, based on the officers' style but without lapels. The regulations specified the coat as blue with blue cuffs, blue standing collar bearing a white patch, buttons like those of Warrant Officers but apparently smaller (three to each cuff and pocket), with white lining, breeches and waistcoat.

George Keith Elphinstone,
ultimately Viscount Keith
(1746–1823), in the 1795
dress uniform of a vice-
admiral with two
epaulette-stars and two
cuff rings. (Engraving by
W. Holl after J. Hoppner)

taken from where it hung in his cabin, it was left upon his table).

Light smallswords were carried for ceremonial occasions and by senior officers, with functional 'fighting swords' used at sea; initially there were no regulations governing the design of either. Apart from the civilian smallsword, a popular pattern from the late 18th century was the straight-bladed spadroon, similar to the army's so-called 1786 pattern, a handsome weapon generally with a cushion- or urn-shaped pommel, a single-bar knuckle bow and short quillon, and usually a bone or ivory grip often inset with a metal locket bearing a crowned anchor. A popular version had five balls cast into the centre of the knuckle bow, hence the term 'five-ball hilt'. The scabbard was black leather with metal throat locket and chape, all fittings being gilded. A plainer version of more robust construction made a useful 'fighting sword', but otherwise these were often curved. Hilts of 'fighting swords' varied from those like that of the spadroon to single-bar stirrup hilts, some resembling the 1796 light cavalry sabre, to two- or three-bar semi-basket hilts, sometimes with a lion-head pommel. Another version was based upon the army's 1803 flank company sabre, with an anchor device incorporated in the single-bar guard—conceivably a pattern used by the Royal Marines. A pattern known to have been presented to officers by the Duke of Clarence incorporated the curious flat-topped pommel of the 10th Light Dragoons' regimental sword.

A regulation sword for officers is mentioned in documents of August 1805, but it is likely that this pattern was established earlier, for in April 1805 medical officers were ordered to carry the 'established' pattern. The August 1805 order mentions two variations: an ornamented sword for the ranks of commander and above, and a plain sword for lieutenants, midshipmen and warrant officers. Evidently it was a straight-bladed weapon with a gilt stirrup hilt, often with langets bearing an embossed fouled anchor, or a crowned anchor, the crown perhaps added in 1812 as on the buttons. The 'ornamented' pattern was presumably that with an ivory or bone grip bound with gilt wire, and a gilt lion-head pommel; and the plain version that with a black fish-skin grip bound with gilt wire, and a plain pommel. Extant examples with black grip and lion-head pommel may have been an unofficial variation carried by lieutenants. The regulations appear not to have been enforced strictly, and many officers continued to carry unofficial patterns, although enough examples of the presumed regulation pattern still exist to suggest that its use was widespread.

A considerable number of swords were presented to officers to recognize a victory or act of heroism, but these were rarely if ever carried on any but the grandest ceremonial occasions. The earlier presentations were mostly superbly decorated smallswords, e.g. those awarded by the City of London, of which 20 were given to naval officers during the Napoleonic Wars, the first to St. Vincent in 1797. They existed in 100- and 200-guinea versions, graded according to the rank of the recipient; for Camperdown, for

Sir John Jervis, Earl St. Vincent (1735–1823). This engraving by Robinson after John Hoppner, painted apparently in 1809, shows the 1795 dress uniform with the three cuff rings of an admiral, with the Gold Medal for St. Vincent and the ribbon and breast star of the Order of the Bath. The telescope is typical of the period.

example, Duncan received a 200-guinea sword and his subordinate Sir Richard Onslow one of 100 guineas. The hilts were enamelled (Duncan's bore a picture of his flagship *Venerable* on the grip, and views of the battle on the shell guards); and the more expensive versions, as presented to Duncan and to Nelson for Aboukir Bay, were inset with diamonds. Not all the City's swords were of this pattern: Capt. Thomas Hardy received a sword with a straight, flat blade (not the diamond-sectioned blade of the small-swords) and a curious mock-classical, highly carved, silver-gilt stirrup hilt.

A bizarre design was presented to Nelson by the Egyptian Club (formed of captains of the victorious fleet at Aboukir Bay), with the entire grip and pommel in the form of a gold crocodile, with an oval enamel view of the battle inset into the grip; apparently some club members had gilt-brass copies made for themselves.

Most famous of the presentation swords were those awarded from 1803 by the Patriotic Fund at Lloyd's, similar in design to the 1796 light cavalry sabre. These magnificent weapons had a gilt-bronze stirrup hilt styled as the club of Hercules, wrapped

with a coiled serpent (representing wisdom), the quillons styled as fasces (representing the state), and the pommel and backstrap as the skin of the Nemean lion. The blued and gilded blade bore a panel recording the incident for which the sword was presented. Swords of £30 value were awarded to midshipmen, mates and marine lieutenants, with black leather scabbards with gilt mounts bearing engraved naval and classical trophies; £50 swords (intended for lieutenants, although 15 were awarded to East India Company captains, nine to marine officers, three to army officers and one to a master) had embossed gilt scabbards with black leather inserts. £100 swords, of which 39 were presented, were intended for captains and commanders (two each went to lieutenants and to army officers, and one to a commodore of the East India Company); their gilt scabbards had blue velvet inserts and serpent-shaped suspension loops instead of the usual rings. A fourth type was the 'Trafalgar' pattern, 29 £100 swords presented to commanders of ships at that battle, four to lieutenants and the remainder to captains.

From about 1790 naval sword knots had a gold lace strap with longitudinal blue lines, a flat tassel bearing an embroidered anchor within a roped oval, and gold cord and bullion fringe. The knots of Lloyd's swords were mixed gold and blue cord with 'round' tassels, a style which seems to have become increasingly popular towards the end of the Napoleonic Wars: Lane's portrait of Broke shows one upon an ordinary dress sword, and others appear in Copley's 1815 portrait of Sir Edward Berry (who received a Lloyd's 'Trafalgar' sword) and Beechey's portrait of Duckworth. An intermediate style is shown in Oliver's portrait of Capt. James Newman Newman, c.1801, a gold lace strap with interwoven blue lines supporting two 'round' gold tassels with blue diagonal stripes and long gold fringe.

The naval dirk was a short and originally straight-bladed dagger generally associated with midshipmen, but was also carried by officers, though rarely shown in contemporary pictures; an exception is Romney's

Sir John Orde Bt. (1751–1824) in the undress uniform of an admiral (three epaulette stars), showing an example of the undress coat with a button on each side of the standing collar, and the lapels partially turned back. (Engraving by S. W. Reynolds after George Romney, published 1811)

portrait of Admiral George Darby, 1783, where a dirk is shown carried on slings. Designs varied widely, some hilts matching that of the 'five-ball' spadroon; a pattern probably slightly later had a curved blade, perhaps copied from French or Danish designs. Grips were often chequered or reeded ivory or bone, often with a lion-head pommel; rarer examples with a crocodile-head pommel may advert to the Egyptian Club. Occasionally a length of chain connected the pommel to the forward quillon, forming an ornamental chain knuckle-bow, and pommel-rings on some weapons suggest the use of sword knots. Scabbards were usually either leather with gilt mounts, or of decorated metal. The effectiveness of the dirk as a weapon, however, must be doubted: 'Flexible Grummet', writing in the *United Service Journal* in 1834, referred to his as 'a tenpenny nail'!

The commonest sword suspension was in a frog upon a narrow waist belt, often in black leather and fastened by a gilt S-shaped hook with plain or lion-mask bosses, worn beneath the coat and waistcoat and almost entirely concealed in many contemporary pictures. Less commonly, the belt is shown over the coat; regulations issued by the Duke of Clarence in 1814 (without Admiralty sanction) specified that when breeches were worn the belt should be under the coat but over the waistcoat, and over the coat when pantaloons were worn. Suspension by slings from the waist belt appears to have become popular in the first decade of the 19th century, as depicted, for example, in Stroehling's portrait of Cochrane in undress uniform. The design of belt was unregulated; varieties included that shown in Lane's portrait of Sir Philip Broke, black with gold embroidered Greek key pattern, and an extant belt which belonged to Admiral Sir William Cornwallis is made of blue silk. The belt and slings supplied with the Patriotic Fund swords were either black leather, or leather covered with blue velvet, with gold wire edges and an undulating central line, and a circular gilt clasp.

Probably more common until the introduction of the 1805 regulation sword with waist belt was a broad belt over the right shoulder, worn over the coat or under the coat and over the waistcoat, often depicted as black leather with an oval plate. This seems to have been used more by junior officers, and perhaps for the 'fighting swords' of others. The design of plate was unregulated, and it is probably impossible to differ-

The 1795 regulation captain's dress coat is illustrated in this unsigned engraving; although only sketched in, just visible is cuff lace of the variety with a peaked upper edge. The decoration is the Naval Gold Medal on its blue-edged white ribbon.

entiate between some naval plates and the early plates of marines. An apparently common pattern was gilt, bearing a crowned fouled anchor, either engraved or struck, sometimes with an ornamental border, as shown in the pattern-book reproduced by Edward Almack as *Regimental Badges Worn in the British Army One Hundred Years Ago*, London 1900, the designs in which appear to pre-date about 1809. A second example features a beaded border and a sloping fouled anchor within a crowned oval Garter. Other recorded examples bear the name of a ship; the inscription 'British Navy' over an anchor, with a cartouche bearing two dolphins over a trident and palm branch; a fouled anchor within a crowned wreath of palm and laurel, upon an oval surrounded by a 'fish scale' pattern; and a crowned fouled anchor upon an oval backed by a naval trophy of arms, including the White Ensign and a trident, with a roped rim.

Thomas Cochrane (1775–1860), perhaps the most renowned naval captain of his generation. This engraving shows an undress coat with standing collar, plain hat, and an excellent depiction of typical neck-wear – a deep black neck-cloth concealing most of the shirt collar, with the collared waistcoat visible inside the coat.

Seamen

Seamen of the Royal Navy had no prescribed uniform until 1857; earlier, they provided their own clothing, and whilst there were distinctive nautical styles they applied equally to merchant seamen. Such clothing could be purchased ashore, but more convenient were the 'slops' from the ship's purser's store, supplied originally via the Navy Slop Office, established 1756. Such clothing was either ready-made or cut and sewn by the men themselves from bolts of fabric; skilled tailors among a crew would make their messmates' clothing in return for payment in 'grog', so that after a tailoring session there might be some drunkenness aboard ship. This production of 'slop' clothing did impose some degree of uniformity, albeit almost accidentally, originating simply from bulk purchase of material rather than deliberate attempts at uniformity.

The nautical style developed for reasons of utility, and included a tail-less jacket, often with a 'mariner's cuff' which by means of a buttoned flap could be turned back for work. Jackets were single- or double-breasted, sometimes with additional rows of buttons; by the mid-18th century blue was becoming the almost universal colour for the jacket. Under the jacket was worn a waistcoat with one or two rows of buttons, and under that a shirt. Checked shirts were so popular that apparently they came to be regarded as the mark of a seaman; a satirical crack in *The Morning Chronicle* of 3 November 1798 reported that Bond Street dandies had taken to wearing 'check shirts and collars to make them look like *sailors*—our readers may suppose, not of the *able-bodied* kind!'. (See also the commentary to Plate G.)

A large handkerchief was usually worn around the neck, which could also be tied around the head as a sweat-band in action. Black was a popular colour, perhaps encouraged by the supply of 'slops' of this shade, but many colours and designs were used.

The original 'slops' were voluminous breeches of about knee length, reminiscent of 17th century 'petticoat breeches', worn with stockings; these continue to be depicted as late as the 1790s, but trousers, first introduced as slop-clothing in the 1720s, were more functional and more popular. Often cut well above the ankle, these had wide legs which allowed them to be rolled up for work; plain light colours and stripes were especially popular. Stockings and buckled shoes would be worn ashore, but at sea bare feet were usual. For details of the mariners' protective 'overskirt', see the commentary to Plate C2.

In the earlier 18th century sailors had generally worn cocked hats, the brims rather small and fastened down to the crown—resembling triangular apple pasties, according to the *London Chronicle* in 1762! By the last decade of the century these had been supplanted by 'round hats'; straw hats, often woven by the sailors, were very popular especially in hot climates, the hats often being tarred for northern regions. The traditional knitted wool or furred 'Monmouth cap' was still used, shown by Atkinson in 1808, for example.

For 'best' wear the sailor lost no opportunity of improving his appearance, by edging the hat and jacket with lace or white tape, adding extra buttons and wearing silver shoe buckles. *The Naval Chronicle* n 1802 recounted a typical story, in which a seaman accosted Admiral Kempenfelt for the name of the tailor who had made the admiral's gold-laced velvet waistcoat. The sailor ordered an identical garment, but specified that the back should also be of the same material; and when he next met the admiral he pulled up the rear of his jacket with a cry of 'Damn me, old boy, no false colours!'.

A degree of uniformity was fashionable among the crews of a captain's or admiral's gig or barge, these crews in a number of cases being recorded as finely dressed, obviously at their commander's expense. This practice was established at least as early as Admiral Lord George Anson (1697–1762) who dressed his gig's crew as Thames watermen, in scarlet jackets with silver sleeve badges and blue silk waistcoats. Such uniforms might include bargemen's caps, cloth or velvet jockey-cap style headdress with an upturned peak. Rear-Admiral Richard Edwards (c.1780) gave his crew blue cloth caps with white piping and a white upturned peak bearing his crest; Lord Hood's equivalent was brown velvet, slightly resembling a light infantry cap with a semi-circular front panel bearing an embroidery of his crest, with a narrow brown velvet peak. Atkinson's print of a gig's crew in 1808 shows a stranger costume, the men wearing longer jackets than usual, petticoat-breeches and stockings, apparently waist-sashes, and a curious, cylindrical headdress with upturned flap, perhaps some type of Monmouth cap. Perhaps the most eccentric of these uniforms was that recorded for the crew of the captain's gig of HMS *Harlequin* (presumably the 18-gun brig-sloop of that name, in service 1813–29), who dressed as harlequins! (See also the commentary to Plate C1).

Although complete uniformity was impossible, partial attempts may have been more common than is often imagined. Orders for the 74-gunner *Mars*, for example, exhorted officers to discourage the purchase of anything other than blue jackets, red, blue or white waistcoats, and white trousers. An early example of a ship's uniform may be that of the 28-gun frigate *Vestal* (in service 1779–1816), which was detailed to convey the Hon. Charles Cathcart as ambassador to China in 1788. He died en route and was buried at Java; a painting of the funeral by the artist Julius Caesar Ibbotson, who accompanied the mission, shows the coffin carried by seamen clad all in white (perhaps the captain's gig crew's dress rather than a sign of mourning), with the remainder in grey-green loose jackets and matching trousers, with 'round hats'. One figure, perhaps a petty officer, wears a tailcoat of the same colour; conceivably the entire crew was outfitted in a uniform manner for this important voyage.

As in the commentary to Plate E2, a description from *The Times* of October 1805 notes the uniform of the crew of HMS *Tribune* including a hat band bearing the name of the ship—a practice still current in the Royal Navy. Not all such inscriptions related to the vessel; on 4 November 1797 *The London Chronicle* reported that the King had cancelled his planned visit to the Nore, for which the seamen 'had mostly bought blue ribands for their hats, with "God save the

Sir Sidney Smith at Acre, wearing the 1795 undress uniform of a captain with the breast star of the Swedish Order of the Sword. Note the rear opening of the cuff, the dark blue Turkish waist sash, Turkish sabre, and the pistol with a carbine stock slung over the shoulder. (Engraving after John Eckstein)

The symbol of the Royal Navy: a fouled anchor, here upon an officer's gilt button of 1812 pattern, at which date the crown was added to the design.

▶ *Gilded waist belt clasp of the Lloyd's Patriotic Fund sabre, bearing a motif which symbolized the role of the Royal Navy during the Napoleonic Wars: Britannia slaying the serpent representing France.*

King"'. An entirely different inscription was reported in *The News* on 19 November 1809, when assistant surgeon George Webb of the 74-gunner *Eagle* (in service from 1803, and not destroyed until 1926) was charged with helping to cause a riot at Covent Garden theatre, at a time of much unrest caused by violent protests against increased prices, by appearing with a placard bearing 'Victory or Death' on the broad side of his cocked hat!

Uniform clothing seems not to have been restricted even to the crews of warships. *The Gentleman's Magazine* of June 1806, reporting the funeral of Field-Marshal the Duke of Argyll, described the dress of the crews of the two revenue-vessels which attended: the boat's crew of *Princess Elizabeth* were 'dressed in nankeen, with crapes round their hats', and the crew of *Prince William Henry*, which formed a guard of honour, were 'dressed in white frocks, with black velvet caps trimmed with silver'. Specific clothing could be regulated for such an occasion: e.g. the seamen who paraded at Nelson's funeral were ordered to wear blue jackets, white trousers, a black crape around the arm and a gold medal for Trafalgar at the neck. Fairburn's engraving of the event shows both seamen and marines with large black crapes tied around their hats.

Hairstyles were not regulated, but queues were common, often of considerable length and bound with black ribbon (Capt. Brenton noted that a long queue, like a lion's tail, was the mark of a 'thoroughbred' seaman); in the navy these were known as pigtails, a term also used to describe plugs of tobacco. Facial hair was not worn, although Dighton shows sideburns of considerable length. It was stated that only Americans wore earrings: a letter

in *The Gentleman's Magazine* in 1814 recalled British officer remarking to an American in his crew who was wearing such ornaments, 'What are you Are you a man or a woman?'.

Officers wore queues at least until the middle o the period under review; but apparently these wer not compulsory, as even early portraits of senio officers show hair lightly powdered and curled at th sides, but without a queue, and quite early portrait show the use of short hair.

Weapons

Weapons were issued to a ship rather than t individuals, but cutlasses could be carried in a frog from a leather shoulder belt (see Plate I4); the seaman portrayed as a supporter for Nelson's arms wa shown wearing a narrow waist belt supporting a cutlass at the right, with two pistols on either side o what appears to be a small, frontal cartridge box Aboard ship it was more likely that weapons were distributed about the decks, to be grabbed when necessary.

The regulation cutlass was produced by a number of manufacturers, and it is not certain that al were of the same exact pattern. That used in the late 18th century commonly had a wide, straight, single-edged 29in. blade with a spear point and a fuller next to the rear edge; a wooden grip with a sheet of iron rolled around it and soldered into a tube; and an iron guard manufactured in a single piece, with 'two-disc' or 'figure-of-eight' configuration, one 'disc' being the guard at the base of the blade and the other one the knuckle bow.

An improved design from about 1804 had a wider, unfullered blade, a more accentuated 'figure-

as there would be little fixing of bayonets to damage the wood (although bayonets were provided for Sea Service muskets from 1752). There were also 'Short Sea Service' muskets, probably assembled from old material, with a barrel length of about 26 inches. Sea Service muskets were classified as 'black' or 'bright': blackened barrels were used to prevent corrosion at sea, and it has been speculated that the bright-barrelled weapons were for marine use, although the presence of 10,000 of each in stores in 1757 perhaps suggests a wider use of the 'bright' version. At the beginning of the period under review a 74-gunner typically carried some 230 muskets (excluding those of marines), only one-fifth being blackened; by 1797 the number was reduced to 130, all 'black'. Their accuracy was poor, largely precluding deliberate sharpshooting; indeed, one writer in the *United Service Journal* (1839) averred that no attempt was made to single out the enemy's officers as targets, which was regarded as an unfair tactic—unlike the French, who 'were ahead of us in cunning means and appliances to destroy life'.

◀ *cast metal shoulder belt plate, perhaps of a warrant officer, of manufacture less fine than might be expected of an officer's plate.*

▶ *A rare example of officer's engraved shoulder belt plate, bearing not only the king's cypher and nautical symbols but also the name of the ship, Proserpine, a name borne by two fifth-rates and a sixth-rate between 1777 and 1809.*

of-eight' guard, and a ribbed grip shaped to the contours of the hand. A suggested further improvement of 1814, apparently with a larger hilt and a blade curved at the end, was not put into production. Other extant types of cutlass or hanger are variations or weapons carried by merchant seamen. Although somewhat crude, the cutlass was doubtless an effective weapon for hand-to-hand conflict.

Other bladed weapons included boarding pikes with triangular-sectioned heads, also used by landing parties; and boarding axes or tomahawks, which usually had a spike at the rear of a curved blade.

The 'Sea Service Musket' was based upon the army's 'Brown Bess' but considerably cheaper in manufacture, retaining wooden ramrods until about 1820 (these did not corrode in the salt air, as did iron), and without the brass cap on the fore-end of the stock, which was apparently regarded as unnecessary

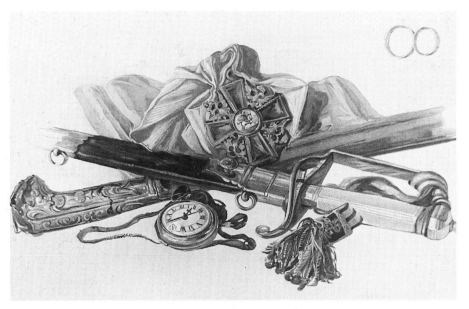

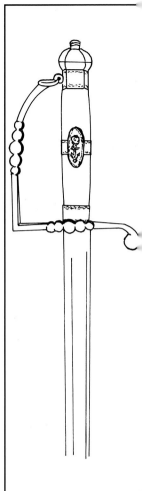

Admiral Duncan's sword, with chequered grip, gilt guard and cushion-shaped pommel, gilt-mounted black leather scabbard and a typical sword knot of gold lace with blue lines, and a gold anchor upon a flat, dark blue 'bell' above the gold bullion and blue silk fringe. Also shown are the sword of Admiral De Winter, captured at

Camperdown; Duncan's watch (found under his pillow at his death); his red-enamelled cross and red ribbon of the Order of St. Alexander Nevski; and the double gold ring worn by Duncan to support a little finger broken in a riot in Edinburgh in June 1792. (Print after W. Gibb)

▶ Typical 'five-ball hilt' spadroon with gilded fittings including cushion-shaped pommel, bone grip with gilt locket engraved with a crowned anchor, and straight 32-inch blade.

Pistols were used at sea for close-quarter combat, being basically a cheaper version of those issued to the army, with heavy brass butt plates suitable for use as a club. An iron belt-hook was affixed to the butt on the reverse side to the lock; barrel length was about 12 ins., and wooden ramrods were used until about 1820, when barrels were reduced to 9 inches. The butt-cap often bore large engraved letters and numbers indicating the position where the pistol was stored, for example 'QD' for quarterdeck, 'F' for forecastle, with sometimes 'P' or 'S' for port or starboard sides.

Weapons which saw more limited use included the musketoon, a flared-mouthed blunderbuss-style weapon, sometimes with a brass barrel: a short-range weapon firing a charge of large shot, this was much more common in the earlier 18th century. Its considerable weight (about 18 lbs.) resulted in it being rested on the gunwale of a ship or longboat to fire, or fitted with a swivel, as in the revenue service.

Some of those remaining in use dated from the late 17th century. A more modern equivalent was the seven-barrelled volley-gun commonly known by the name of the maker, Henry Nock, although it was not his invention, having been proposed to the Board of Ordnance by one James Wilson. Some 500 were contracted for manufacture by Nock in 1780, and a further 100 in 1787, but by the late 1790s they were probably obsolete. Weighing some 12 lbs., measuring 42 ins. overall, and firing all seven barrels simultaneously, the volley-gun must have been a formidable weapon; but would have been unpopular for use in ships' fighting-tops due to the danger of setting the sails alight by the flame of firing, a danger which also discouraged the use of ordinary musketry from such a position. Doubtless the volley-gun's greatest value would have been in firing upon a closely packed boarding party.

ROYAL MARINES

The corps of Marines, later Royal Marines, traced its antecedents to 1664, and in seniority ranked between the 49th and 50th Regiments of Foot. Regularly enlisted like the army, not by impressment, the marines provided ships with a force of troops capable of fighting as infantry on land, of manning guns aboard ship, and of acting as marksmen and in close combat at sea. A subsidiary duty was to discourage or suppress mutiny among the seamen: aboard ship the marines' quarters separated those of the officers from those of the sailors (though a number of marines were involved in the Nore and Spithead mutinies). The value of the marines was recognized by the granting of the title 'Royal Marines' on 29 April 1802; St. Vincent, who was instrumental in securing the award of this honour, remarked that even this was less than they deserved, for he had never known an occasion in which they had not exceeded everything required of them in loyalty, courage and honour: they were, he claimed, the country's true sheet-anchor in time of danger.

The corps grew in strength from 15,000 in 1795, 20,000 in 1797 and 30,000 in 1805, to a total regulated at 31,400 from 1808 to 1814. Organization was based upon three 'Divisions', numbered 1–3 but almost invariably designated by their location—Chatham, Portsmouth and Plymouth respectively; a 4th Division was created at Woolwich in 1805. In that year, for example, the Chatham Division comprised 47 companies plus the 1st Artillery Company, Portsmouth 48 plus the 2nd Artillery Company, Plymouth 48 plus the 3rd Artillery Company, and Woolwich 30 plus the 4th Artillery Company. Companies were numbered but were not grouped consecutively save for the Woolwich Division, of which the companies were those numbered 144–173, with nos. 174–183 added in July 1808. Expansion of the corps was achieved partly by the increase of company size, but mainly by the creation of new companies.

Establishment varied: from January 1801, for example, each company was ordered to comprise 1 captain, 2 first lieutenants, 2 second lieutenants, 8 sergeants, 8 corporals, 6 drummers and 140 privates. Following the Peace of Amiens the corps was reduced from an authorized 30,000 men to 12,000, in 100

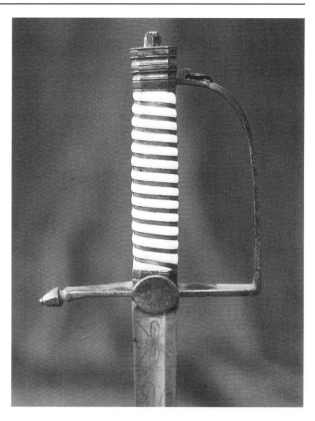

A typical officer's 'fighting sword' or spadroon, with ivory grip bound with copper wire and a plain steel hilt, bearing no obvious naval identification except for the figure of Britannia (and 'GR') etched on the 32-inch straight blade.

companies, with officers as above but with 6 sergeants, 6 corporals, 4 drummers and 100 privates. In June 1803 this was increased to 8 sergeants, 8 corporals, 5 drummers and 130 privates, and in 1808 to the same but with 140 privates. Reductions began in June 1814 with the discharge of foreigners, the infirm, those aged over 40 or under 5ft. 3½ins. in height. From 183 companies plus four of artillery in 1808, in December 1815 the corps was reduced to 80 companies and only 6,000 men. Each Division had a Grenadier and a Light Company until 1 November 1804, when these distinctions were abolished.

In practice, companies were merely administrative units reduced to skeleton cadres; the majority of men were allocated to ships roughly as indicated in Table A, the proportion of marines to seamen increasing slightly over the period. As men were usually sent to ships in small drafts, the company identity bore no relation to the composition of

An officer's or warrant officer's 'fighting sword', a workmanlike hanger with slightly curved 25-inch blade, reeded bone grip, and gilt hilt and scabbard lockets.

▼ *An example of the ornamented version of the 1805 sword, for senior ranks, with gilt hilt including lion-head pommel and chequered ivory grip with gilt wire bands. The presence of the crown above the anchor on the langets may suggest a date of 1812 or later, at which time that motif was added to the buttons. Length of the straight blade was generally about 32 inches.*

detachments aboard ship. Field officers served at sea so rarely that they had no scheme for higher pay when afloat, as had all the lower ranks. Between 1760 and 1837 naval officers were appointed to the ranks of generals and colonels; in 1805, for example, the corps' general was Admiral Lord Bridport, the lieutenant-general Admiral the Earl of St. Vincent, and the major-general Admiral Lord Gardner. Nelson was a colonel of the Chatham Division from 1795.

A considerable number of foreigners were enlisted: of recruits received at Portsmouth in the first half of 1805, for example, over nine per cent were foreigners, a proportion rising to almost 14 per cent when militia volunteers are excluded. Recruiting stations were opened in Malta and the West Indies, but the enlistment of foreigners was stopped in 1810.

For service ashore, marines and naval landing parties were usually drawn from ships' companies, even when serving in battalion-sized units like that in Cavan's brigade in Egypt in 1801. In September 1810, however, the 1st Marine Battalion was created specifically for service in the Peninsular War, two companies and the Divisional artillery being provided by Plymouth and one company each from the Chatham and Portsmouth Divisions. Each company comprised the best men available, including one captain, two lieutenants, 80 privates (of whom ten were allowed to be foreigners, providing only Germans were selected), and NCOs in proportion; eventually the unit comprised 19 officers (including two majors) and 503 other ranks. It served in garrison in Lisbon, and was sent home to recruit to 500 rank and file in January 1812; and was subsequently sent to the north coast of Spain, where it performed a number of landings, including that at Santander (which became the army's base for re-supply in the later Peninsular War). A 2nd Battalion was sent to Santander in August 1812, of which each company comprised one captain, two lieutenants, four sergeants, five corporals, two drummers and 55 privates.

In January 1813 both battalions were detailed for service in North America, each being made up to two majors, eight captains, 16 lieutenants, 34 sergeants, 32 corporals, 16 drummers and 640 privates; plus an artillery company of one captain, four lieutenants, four corporals, six bombardiers, two drummers and 60 gunners; and a battalion staff of an adjutant, a paymaster, and a surgeon and assistant. A 3rd

1: Admiral, undress, c.1794
2: Captain (3 years' post), full dress, c.1794
3: Lieutenant, full dress, c.1794
4: Officer, Marines, c.1794

A

1: Admiral, full dress, 1794
2: Captain, undress, 1794
3: Lieutenant, undress, 1794
4: Officer, 2nd Foot, 1794

WRJ. 92

B

1: Captain's gig crew, c.1795
2: Seaman, c.1795
3: Seaman, c.1795
4: Private, Marines, c.1795

3

2

1

4

WRy. 92

C

1: Captain, undress, 1797
2: Midshipman, 1797
3: Seaman, 1797
4: Private, 69th Foot, 1797

WRY. 92

1: Seaman ashore, c.1805
2: Seaman, HMS Tribune, 1805
3: Lieutenant, undress, c.1805
4: Officer, Royal Marines, c.1805

WRY. 92

1: Vice-admiral Nelson, undress, 1805
2: Vice-admiral Collingwood, full dress, 1805
3: Captain Hardy, full dress, 1805
4: Private, Royal Marines, 1805

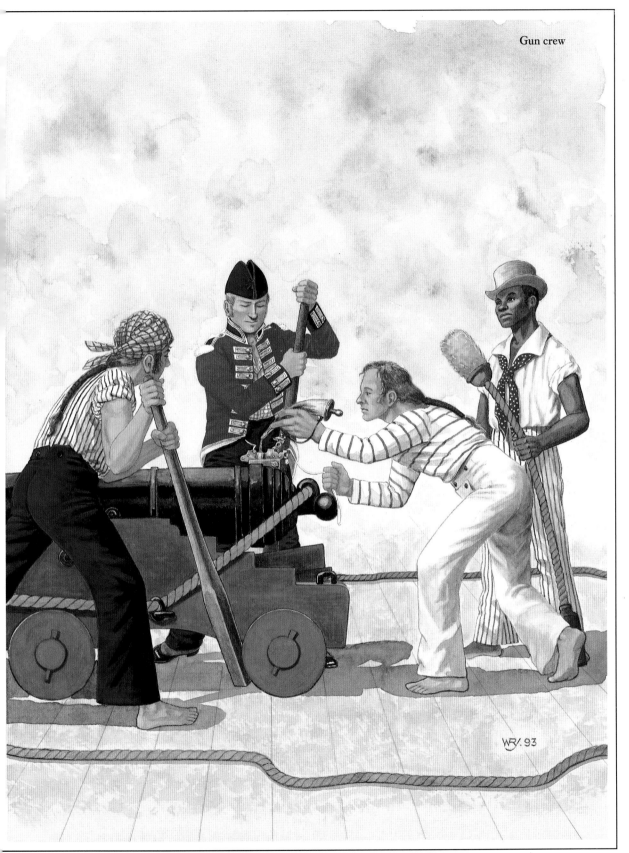

1: Cook
2: Ship's boy
3: Carpenter
4: Boatswain's mate

WRY. 92

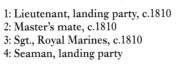

1: Lieutenant, landing party, c.1810
2: Master's mate, c.1810
3: Sgt., Royal Marines, c.1810
4: Seaman, landing party

WRy. 92

1: Master, c.1807
2: Surgeon, c.1807
3: Seaman, landing party, 1807
4: Officer, Royal Marines, c.1807

WRY. 92

J

1: Junior captain, c.1810
2: Master, 1812
3: Midshipman, c.1812
4: Volunteer

1: Vice-admiral, full dress, c.1813
2: Captain, full dress, c.1813
3: Lieutenant, undress, c.1813
4: Boatswain, post-1807

WRV. 93

Battalion was formed in February 1813, partially from men lately serving in Holland, of ten companies of 100 other ranks each plus an 80-strong artillery company; this also went to North America.

The original battalions were broken up to provide crews for the gunboats on the lakes; the 3rd Battalion became the 2nd, and in September a new 3rd was formed from companies of the 2nd and three companies of 'Colonial Marines' raised in North America from escaped slaves; the 1st Battalion was also reformed. The 'Colonial Marines' proved to be especially fine recruits, 'good men and true' according to a writer in the *United Service Journal* (1840), 'prime favourites amongst our soldiers and sailors'. At the conclusion of the War of 1812 the 3rd Battalion was disbanded in Bermuda and the others returned to England; the 'Colonial Marines' received free land-grants in Canada in return for their exemplary service, having found the 'perfect freedom—that freedom which the vaunted "Land of Liberty" denied them'.

Royal Marines uniform

Although the marines came under the aegis of the Admiralty and had their uniforms supplied by the Navy Board, their dress was like that of the infantry, including a red coat with white facings, white smallclothes, and bicorn. The issue of army-style grenadier and light infantry caps was authorized in 1786 (perhaps before), and approval of fur grenadier caps was confirmed in May 1792—doubtless the army's 1768-pattern cap. In September 1797 hat-feathers were confirmed as company distinctions: white-over-red for battalion companies, white for grenadiers and green for light infantry. Throughout the period, however, it is possible that minor differences in dress existed between Divisions: black plumes, for example, seem to have been used by the Chatham Division.

For officers' uniform, see the commentary to Plate A4. All appear to have worn two epaulettes, with rank distinctions noted as early as April 1797 in orders for the Chatham Division: majors to have a gold star on the straps, lieutenant-colonels two, and colonels three. Orders of the same date abolished silver-laced hats (plain hats may have been worn for ordinary service), and in place of silver introduced gold and crimson corner-tassels, as worn by Line

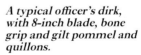

A typical officer's dirk, with 8-inch blade, bone grip and gilt pommel and quillons.

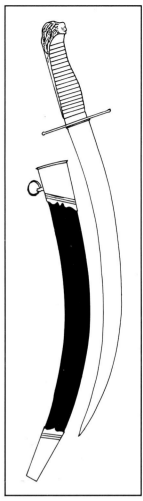

Curved dirk with gilt lion-head pommel and quillons, ribbed ivory grip, black leather scabbard with gilt fittings; 14-inch blade.

officers. Gorgets were to remain unchanged: silver, bearing the royal arms below an anchor, with a spray of laurel below. The crimson waist-sash was generally worn under the coat, until in June 1798 it was ordered to be worn outside, presumably to conform with the latest practice of wearing the lapels closed. In August 1798 Plymouth Divisional Orders noted that sashes of a new pattern were to be worn over the left shoulder, possibly a short-lived fashion.

A number of officers' shoulder belt plates are recorded, and sometimes confused with plates likely to be of naval origin. Before 1797 it appears that oval silver plates were worn, bearing an anchor; other recorded plates, with possible marine provenance, have a gilt crowned anchor with laurel surround and a roped border, the devices upon a ground of blue and red cloth or brown velvet. In April 1797 it was ordered that plates should be 'square' (actually with rounded corners) bearing 'a lion and crown' (i.e. a lion atop a crown, from the royal crest); an extant example has a roped border. Officers' buttons were silver, bearing a fouled anchor within a wreath, with a scalloped edge; an order of June 1798 stated that they were to be convex. The other ranks' button was pewter, bearing an incised fouled anchor.

The grant of the title 'Royal' occasioned a major change in uniform, with the adoption of the appropriate blue facings. This order was dated between 1 and 6 May 1802, but it was noted that the alteration would not take place until the king's birthday (4 June); and for reasons of economy, the new uniform was to be reserved for dress parades until the old uniform was worn out. The alteration to a short-tailed, single-breasted jacket of infantry style for the rank and file appears to have taken place already: it is shown, with white facings and infantry-style lace loops, in De Loutherbourg's painting of the cutting-out of the French ship *La Chevrette* in July 1801.

At the same time as the change in facing colour, officers adopted gold instead of silver lace, captains and subalterns conforming to army practice by wearing an epaulette on the right shoulder only. Gilt buttons for officers were confirmed on 24 May, placed in pairs (as they may have been before, being shown thus in a portrait of the white-faced uniform), with gold loops for dress uniform, including a loop and button on each side of the collar. A tailor's pattern describes officers' turnback badges in the shape of an embroidered heart. Officers' metalwork changed from silver to gilt, the belt plate retaining the previous shape and lion-on-crown device; the gorget

Devis' painting 'The Death of Nelson' shows the scene in the cockpit of HMS Victory *at Trafalgar; Dr. Beatty (holding Nelson's hand) is distinguished by his embroidered collar loop of a ship's surgeon; his coat cuffs are turned back for work, and he wears buff or light brown breeches and Hessian boots.*

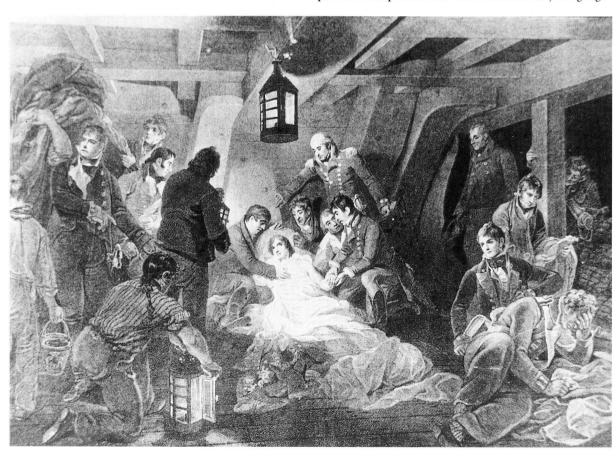

bore the royal arms over a shield bearing an anchor, over a laurel spray. Buttons were now flat, gilt, with a relief design of 'Royal Marines' over a fouled anchor, over a laurel spray; the other ranks' version was similar, in pewter. A tailor's pattern mentions buttons according to Division, but distinctive designs are not recorded. The lace worn by the rank and file was apparently unchanged by the grant of the 'Royal' title, remaining white with red and blue lines, the loops square-ended and in pairs.

The bicorn was replaced by a black 'round hat' made of lacquered felt, with a black cockade and corps button at the left, with a short tuft above. Orders of March 1799 noted company distinctions: battalion companies, white band and brim-edge, black looping (from brim to crown), and white-over-red tuft; grenadiers, white band, looping and tuft, black brim-binding; light companies, as grenadiers but green tuft. The painting of the boarding of *La Chevrette* shows these hats with white binding but black tufts, perhaps the plume of the Chatham Division. An officer in this painting appears to wear a 'Tarleton' helmet with black crest, white metal fittings and apparently a white plume. Apart from an experimental issue of 'caps' (perhaps shakos for the artillery, see below) ordered in May 1812, the headdress remained the same for the remainder of the period, apart from the abolition of flank company distinctions in 1804. For officers, who continued to wear the bicorn, see Plate J4.

In March 1810 officers' rank badges were altered to conform to those introduced for the army: company officers to wear an epaulette on the right shoulder only, with bullion fringe for captains and plain fringe for subalterns; field officers to wear two epaulettes, bearing a star for majors, crown for lieutenant-colonels, and crown and star for colonels. In June 1812 it was ordered that officers' coats should be made to fasten across the breast; presumably this introduced the short-tailed jacket as for the infantry. Paymasters and medical staff wore neither epaulettes nor sash, and had a waist belt instead of a shoulder belt; and from April 1809 adjutants wore an epaulette on the right shoulder and a laced strap on the left. Bicorns and long boots were ordered for attendance at court. For NCO distinctions, see the commentary to Plate I3.

White breeches and black gaiters were probably

Although pre-dating the French Revolutionary Wars, this cartoon shows a British 'tar' already wearing striped long trousers. A seam is visible on the inside of the jacket cuff, enabling it to be rolled up for work; the head-dress is a forerunner of the 'round hat', a tricorn with narrow brim. The seaman in the doorway of the inn wears the protective overskirt.

restricted to 'dress' occasions (there are also references to white gaiters for parade), and in 1802 it was noted that the breeches were so tight that on occasion none could be found to fit grenadiers, who in army fashion were generally the largest men. Trousers were probably the ordinary wear on service, one of the earliest references being a note that from 1801 marines were permitted to purchase warmer woollen 'pantaloons' for service in the North Sea. Contemporary illustrations show white or blue trousers, or white 'gaiter-trousers'; Dighton shows officers in blue trousers and other ranks in white. An order of December 1808 specified that trousers and pantaloons should be dyed 'fast blue' rather than grey, presumably in use before; and in December 1815 it was ordered that 'mixed cloth' (i.e. grey) trousers and half-gaiters should be worn, instead of the blue trousers then in use.

Greatcoats were issued initially only for sentries;

those issued in 1786 had a cape and were made of 'blue fearnought', but the commandant at Portsmouth had some coats made of light drab cloth as used by the artillery; drab seems to have been the standard colour until orders of October 1813 specified that officers' and other ranks' greatcoats should be like those of the Line infantry, i.e. grey. Earlier, officers appear to have worn blue coats with a cape, and red collar.

Hair was worn in a 'queue' until these were abolished by an order of 18 September 1808; in 1796 NCOs and other ranks were ordered to powder their hair, but this order was soon rescinded.

For work aboard ship, marines bought the same 'slop' clothing as the seamen, but attempts were usually made to maintain their distinction. In action it was probably usual for marines to wear their red jackets; but Lieutenant Roteley of HMS *Victory* described how in the excitement of Trafalgar the marines on the gun-decks had discarded their jackets and were virtually indistinguishable from the seamen, in checked shirts and blue trousers, all 'working like horses'. Checked shirts are mentioned as early as 1775 (an issue of one checked to four white shirts per man), with an old hat and jacket for 'sea kit'. Other references suggest the use of white undress jackets of army style: these were mentioned in orders for HMS *Blenheim*, to be worn with white trousers and pipeclayed canvas caps in fine weather between the hours of 8am and 8pm. An undress cap of this style is shown in Drummond's painting of Camperdown, a somewhat shapeless, bag-like construction; see Plate G for another. During the American War of Independence, marines had worn 'light clothing' for hot climates, with linen lining instead of wool, raven duck smallclothes, and thread stockings, but it was noted in 1798 that only 500 sets of this uniform had been produced for the war then in progress.

Weapons and equipment

Equipment was of army style, including white leather shoulder belts and black leather cartridge box, which bore a brass eight-pointed star badge, with 'GR' in the centre within a circlet inscribed 'Per mare per terram'. The shoulder belt plate from c.1802 was oblong, brass, and bore a crowned fouled anchor with a scroll above inscribed 'Royal Marines' and a laurel spray below. There is also evidence for the use of 'divisional' plates, one oblong brass example bearing a fouled anchor with script letters 'RM' by the shank and 'PD' at the base, presumably indicating either Plymouth or Portsmouth Division. Charles Hamilton Smith, however, shows an oval plate. Grenadiers had a grenade insignia on their belts and pouches.

Although the equipment was of army style, marines were often not fully equipped for service on land; at the Cape in 1795, for example, the marine unit had to borrow 78 camp kettles from the 78th Regt., and whilst the infantry had spare 'magazines' fitted to their belts to hold extra cartridges (60 per man), the marines had no such extra pouches and carried their additional cartridges, tied up in paper packets of ten, in their knapsacks. The marines brought their hammocks ashore, but were ordered to return them to their ships and carry only a blanket for the campaign; apparently both the marine and naval

'A Son of the Ocean'; a seaman in a typical 'best' uniform, including shoes with huge gilt buckles, a blue jacket bound with white lace, red waistcoat, checked shirt, white trousers, spotted red neckerchief, and a 'round hat' with a gilt-buckled band. (Engraving by C. Knight after H. Singleton, published January 1794)

battalions had been issued with haversacks and blankets. In 1812 it was recorded that extra musket slings were issued to the 1st Battalion to improve the carriage of the knapsack, perhaps for use as a waist belt to hold the equipment in place.

Marines carried the Sea Service musket, or perhaps one of the 'Land' patterns; not until December 1812 was it ordered that barrels should be browned in army style. Officers' swords were like those of the army, an order of April 1797 noting that the silver-hilted swords of 'old established' type (probably the 1786-style spadroon) would henceforth have a crimson and gold knot; presumably prior to that date the sword knots were in the corps' lace-colour, silver. Possibly the 1796 infantry pattern sword was adopted later, and a known example carried by a marine field officer is like the 1796 heavy cavalry undress pattern. In December 1805 Plymouth orders instructed officers to wear waist belts, but in December 1810 white waist belts were ordered to be restricted to general and staff officers, all others to have white shoulder belts $2\frac{3}{4}$ins. wide, mounted officers' belts to have slings.

Each Division had a stand of colours, and it was noted that in December 1800 new ones were supplied with the cross of St. Patrick added to the Union (presumably on both King's and Regimental Colours, which in army style would have been a large Union, and of regimental colour with a small Union in the upper canton respectively); and upon the grant of blue facings, blue colours were requested, the previous regimental ones apparently having been red. The colours were not taken aboard ship, but it is believed that the Portsmouth Division colours were taken to Spain by the 2nd Battalion.

Royal Marine Artillery

Originally men from the Royal Artillery crewed the mortars and howitzers with which bomb-vessels were armed, a task requiring a level of skill above that of ordinary gunners; but difficulties arose when the artillerymen refused to perform any other duties save the manning of ordnance, so in August 1804 it was ordered that this duty should be transferred to the

Royal Marines. A company of Royal Marine Artillery was formed for each Division, and one for the Woolwich Division in 1805; company strength comprised a captain, 3 first lieutenants, 5 second lieutenants, 8 sergeants, 5 corporals, 8 bombardiers, 3 drummers and 62 gunners.

In addition to crewing bomb-vessels they instructed the other companies in gunnery, to enable ordinary marines to assist the naval gunners; and detachments accompanied the battalions which served in the Peninsula and War of 1812, for which they possessed their own howitzers. They also used rockets, for example against Boulogne in November 1805 and, from land-launchers, at New Orleans.

As their duties tended to soil the ordinary red uniform the artillerymen were permitted to purchase blue jackets and overalls, and in 1811 a blue uniform similar to that of the Royal Artillery was authorized for use both afloat and ashore; blue service uniform was sanctioned for officers in 1812. For the detachments which served in the War of 1812, blue jackets, grey trousers and half-gaiters were issued in March 1814, perhaps like those of the Royal Artillery, i.e. with red facings and yellow lace. The same detach-

Jack bids farewell to his sweetheart: a rare back view of the typical seaman's costume, including a jacket with a vent and two buttons at the rear waist, and 'petticoat-breeches' and stockings.

ment wore 'caps', presumably an army shako, which could have been the 'Belgic' pattern of 1812. The plate sometimes described as the 1816 pattern resembled the shape of the plate commonly worn on the earlier 'stovepipe' shako: it bore a struck design of a crown over a strap inscribed 'Royal Marine Artillery', backed by a trophy of arms and flags and surrounding a fouled anchor, all over a mortar with a pyramid of cannon balls on each side. In October 1816 it was ordered that the Royal Marine Artillery be clothed exactly as for the Royal Artillery, with the exception of headdress and buttons, which were to be those of the Royal Marines.

The army at sea

To compensate for shortages of marines, drafts of army personnel could be assigned temporarily to shipboard duties; but a distinction should be made between soldiers embarked for a specific amphibious

operation and those who became part of the ships' crews. In the former role all manner of troops might be used, as diverse as the 550 Portuguese who assisted the crew of HMS *Confiance* at the capture of Cayenne in January 1809, or the detachment of the Madras European Regiment which assisted the navy's capture of Banda Neira in August 1810.

The use of troops as marines occurred mainly in the early French Revolutionary War. At the 'Glorious First of June', for example, 13 ships carried marines, five ships had detachments of the 2nd Foot, six of the 29th Foot, two of the 25th Foot and two of the 69th Foot. Among regiments which acted as marines during this period were the following infantry units: 1st, 2nd, 11th, 12th, 18th, 25th, 29th, 30th, 50th, 51st, 56th, 63rd, 69th, 86th, 89th, 90th (their 2nd Battalion was drafted into the Marines), 91st, 97th, 118th, Royal York Rangers and Royal Newfoundland Fencibles. Even cavalry regiments could serve as marines: the 12th Light Dragoons served in the Mediterranean in 1795, and at the same time a detachment of 17th Light Dragoons served as marines aboard Pigot's infamous *Hermione*. Service at sea could be prolonged: a detachment of the 25th, for example, spent some five years as marines aboard the 98-gunner *St. George*.

During the 1790s the use of troops as marines declined, although detachments served at St. Vincent—most famously from the 69th, which served on two ships, including Nelson's HMS *Captain*. In 1798 a company of the Scotch Brigade (later 94th) embarked at Madras aboard the 44-gunner *Sybille*, that ship having many of her crew sick; the 23rd served briefly aboard the Channel Fleet in 1800; the 15th aboard Nelson's fleet in the Caribbean in 1805 (although they were disembarked before Trafalgar); and a detachment of the 60th served aboard the brig *Grenada* when it captured the French schooner *Princess Murat* off Martinique in February 1806. *Grenada*'s captain reported of this detachment that 'I cannot sufficiently extol their

A contemporary depiction of a typical seaman: woven straw 'round hat', black handkerchief tied around the neck, dark blue double-breasted jacket with flapped 'mariner's cuff', and flap-fronted white trousers cut with wide ankles to enable them to be rolled up for work at sea. The cudgel is probably also quite typical! (Many contemporary pictures show the trousers very much shorter, exposing the stockings well above the ankle.)

coolness, and strict attention to my direction in action.' Mixed detachments could also be employed: when the captured Spanish polacca *San José* was commissioned under the name HMS *Calpe* in 1801, as no marines were available, 22 men were taken from the Gibraltar garrison, from the Royal Artillery, 5th and 63rd Foot, Cambrian Rangers, and the Argyll, Banffshire and Prince of Wales' Own Fencible regiments, commanded by an officer of the 5th. They remained aboard some months even after the correct complement of marines joined.

Detachments of the Royal Artillery, 49th Foot and 95th Rifles embarked upon the fleet before the battle of Copenhagen (1801), and when the attack was mounted the 49th and Riflemen were distributed among the ships involved to serve as marines. Most unusually, one of their fatalities was a militia captain, James Bawden of the Cornish Miners, who was serving as a volunteer with the 95th.

As with marines, army field officers did not normally serve at sea; for example, it was noted that the Huguenot-descended lieutenant-colonel of the 69th, William Anne Villettes, was exempted from sea service by his rank, and only rejoined his regiment when they reverted to a land role at Toulon.

Landing parties

Operations conducted on land by naval forces included hit-and-run raids by frigates' crews, the creation of naval and marine battalions to serve in an army role, and the crewing of heavy ordnance landed by the fleet to supplement that of the army (for example, the naval siege batteries used at San Sebastian). It was a testimony to the determination of the Royal Navy that landing actions were usually successful, and included some memorable exploits. For example, a landing party of 50 seamen from the 38-gun frigate *Hydra* captured the shore batteries and town of Begu, Catalonia, in August 1807, and held them until the remainder of the crew captured three French polaccas (lateen-rigged Mediterranean craft) in the harbour, for the loss of only one man killed and six wounded.

Despite being trained for service at sea, naval personnel showed considerable resource and skill on land: at the Cape in 1795, for example, it was reported that a light company of seamen commanded by Lieut. Campbell of the sloop *Echo* was no less effective than

The sailor's return: a young seaman returns from a voyage with a hat full of prize-money with which to relieve his impoverished family. The costume shown is typical, a single-breasted jacket with wide sleeves and long trousers ending well above the ankle.

the best trained light infantrymen of the army. In his dispatch reporting the capture of Cuxhaven (8 July 1809) in a typical hit-and-run raid, Capt. Goate of the brig-sloop *Musquito* noted that one reason why the garrison made so little resistance to the landing party was 'from their regularity in forming and marching, that induced the enemy to retreat', obviously believing that the *ad hoc* assembly of seamen and marines were regular troops. Indeed, evidence of the seriousness with which operations on land were taken is the fact that a company of seamen landed at Rio de la Plata in 1806 accorded itself the military-style title 'the Royal Blues'!

The equipment carried by a landing party is shown in Plate J3, and an officer's description of a landing party at Java in 1811 is noted in the text to Plate I4. He noted that the officers carried 'fanciful' weapons, one a 'small bodkin called a dirk', another a Turkish hanger, 'another a species of spit'; the author himself, to accompany his best uniform (his 'ordinary deck jacket' being 'not fit to pay my respects to our friends on shore in') carried a ship's pistol on the right of his belt, a dirk on the left, and a very rusty, brass-

hilted skewer of a sword captured from a French privateer, which had no scabbard and was tucked behind the dirk-belt.

THE PLATES

A1: Admiral, undress uniform, c.1794

This figure, wearing the 1787 undress uniform, is based upon Lemuel Abbott's portrait of Samuel, Lord Hood. The long lapels with 12 loops, extending as low as the upper edge of the pocket, are shown in Abbott's portrait of Alexander Hood, Lord Bridport, painted apparently in 1795. The former portrait depicts the use of a laced hat with undress uniform, and a smallsword which appears to have a colichemarde blade.

A2: Captain of three years' post, full dress, c.1794

Captains' 1787 full dress consisted of a blue coat with white lining, blue standing collar with double gold lace edging; white lapels edged with gold lace with nine buttons on each (although an extant uniform has ten, and portraits suggest an alternative of eight); pockets and white cuffs with three buttons. Captains of 'three years' post' had two lines of lace around the pocket and cuff; those of less than three years, a single line. The sword shown is the common spadroon with 'five-ball' hilt.

A3: Lieutenant, full dress, c.1794

Lieutenants' 1787 dress uniform was like that of the captains, without the gold lace, but with the same buttons. Although not mentioned in the regulations, contemporary pictures show a button and a hole on each side of the collar. Hats were generally unlaced, save for the loop and tassels, but some sources show gold-laced hats; the large cockade is as shown in Mather Brown's painting of the 'Glorious First of June'. Although a waist belt might be worn, this figure has the shoulder belt frequently depicted, with one of a number of designs of plate.

A4: Officer, Marines, c.1794

Marine officers wore scarlet infantry-style uniform with white facings and silver lace; some illustrations show the use of silver lace button-loops in pairs, but others depict embroidered thread loops, possibly the former being for dress uniform. Company distinctions included a button upon a black rose on the turnbacks for battalion companies, and a grenade and button upon a rose for grenadiers; and in May 1797 it was ordered that grenadier officers were to wear a 'fuze' (sic: a grenade badge) on their epaulettes, and light infantry officers a bugle, but no wings. One portrait shows an epaulette strap of silver figure-of-eight lace upon red backing with silver fringe, and others plain silver.

B1: Admiral, full dress, 1794

Based on Mather Brown's painting of Howe at the battle of the 'Glorious First of June', this shows the 1787 full dress coat as described in the text, shown worn by Howe with an unlaced hat. The sword portrayed by Brown appears to be one of Howe's which is still extant, a spadroon-style blade with a knuckle-bow bearing a pierced fouled anchor, and a grip bound with alternating copper and silver wires. L. J. Mosnier's portrait of Lord Rodney, and T. Stuart's of St. Vincent, show an unofficial gold cord strap on the right shoulder, added to hold in place the ribbon of the Order of the Bath.

B2: Captain, undress, 1794

Captains' undress included a blue coat with falling collar and lapels which could be buttoned across. The gold lace loops were square-ended, and included one on each side of the collar and two on each cuff and pocket flap, spaced evenly for senior captains and in threes for junior captains. Loops might be present on both sides of the lapels, to be visible even when the lapels were buttoned over. The figure illustrated has the common pattern of spadroon, and carries a speaking-trumpet.

B3: Lieutenant, undress, 1794

According to the 1787 regulations the undress coat for lieutenants was blue throughout, including lapels (which could be fastened across), plain cuffs and standing collar, all (and skirts and pocket flaps) edged with white piping. The lapels had nine buttons, the cuffs and pockets three, and, as for the dress coat, the collar had a button and hole on each side. The typical 'fighting sword' illustrated is a curved hanger.

B4: Officer, 2nd Foot, 1794

The 2nd (Queen's Royal) Regiment provided detachments to act as marines upon five ships at the 'Glorious First of June' (the flagship *Queen Charlotte*, *Defence*, *Majestic*, *Royal George* and *Russell*). This figure is based upon Mather Brown's painting of the death of Lieut. Neville aboard *Queen Charlotte*; he was one of five sons of the Neville family of Badworth Hall, Yorkshire, who died on active service within a few years—two were killed in the Netherlands and others died of fever in the Mediterranean and Caribbean. Brown depicts the regimental uniform apparently with a folding collar (though it had worn upright collars as early as 1784); and although he

A gun crew in action, showing the ropes and pulley blocks which permitted the gun to be run in and out of the gun-port and controlled recoil. The gun captain (striped shirt, with powder horn slung over the shoulder) orders the gun to be traversed by men using handspikes; the ship's boy (extreme right) carries a prepared cartridge for the next round. To the right is a smouldering match over a water-tub, for use in the event of failure of the gun's flintlock ignition.

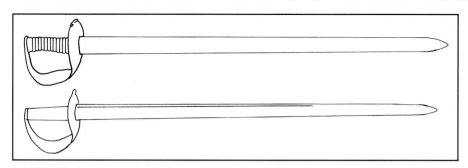

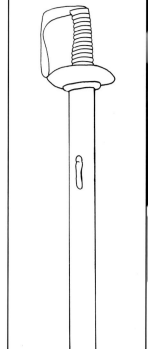

shows officers with an epaulette on the right shoulder only, in the usual way, Neville wears one on his left shoulder, presumably in addition to that on the right—perhaps a flank company distinction (as suggested by the curved sabre). Edward Dayes' print of the regiment depicts a black plume.

C1: Crewman of a captain's gig, c.1795

An example of what is presumably a 'uniform' worn by the members of a captain's gig crew is shown in Dominic Serres' engraving of 1777, including the standard type of bargeman's cap, perhaps black leather, with a front-plate or upturned peak bearing the captain's personal crest. The voluminous 'slops' worn with stockings survived at least until the late 1790s, despite the increasing use of trousers.

C2: Seaman, c.1795

This man wears a checked shirt, apparently typical at this period, and the traditional canvas kilt, overskirt or 'petticoat'. This ancient garment, intended to protect the legs during work aboard ship, probably continued in use until the 1820s, but is depicted only rarely after the turn of the century, suggesting that its use declined; it is shown by Atkinson in 1808, for example.

C3: Seaman, c.1795

Taken from a contemporary print, this shows the rear of the ordinary jacket, and the use of what appears to be a civilian 'round hat'. The low 'round hat' with narrow brim, as worn by figure C2, was probably first created from a tricorn hat with the brim trimmed.

C4: Marine private, c.1795

This figure wears the ordinary Marine uniform, with white facings and without lace at this period.

Cutlasses: 1790s version with rolled iron grip and fullered blade; 1804 type with ribbed iron grip shaped to the hand and a broad, flat blade. Blade lengths were usually about 28 and 30 inches respectively.

1804-style cutlass with a plain black leather scabbard, with no throat-mounting but a brass frog hook.

Westall's painting of Tenerife shows a similar uniform, worn with buff long trousers (by both officers and men), and a flat-brimmed 'round hat' perhaps made from a bicorn with the brim lowered and trimmed.

D1: Captain, undress, 1797

This plate depicts Nelson's boarding party as it might have appeared in his famous exploit at St. Vincent, when the boarding party he led from HMS *Captain* captured two Spanish ships, *San Nicolas* and *San Josef*, crossing the deck of the former to reach the latter ('Nelson's Patent Bridge for Boarding', as it became known!). A coat exists which he reputedly wore at the battle, and in which he was painted by Lemuel Abbott; here he is shown wearing the 1795-pattern captain's undress coat with closed lapels and the stand-and-fall collar shown by contemporary sources. A similar coat, with lapels worn open, is shown in a 1797 portrait by Edridge, with a band of lace around the cuff, obviously added after Nelson's promotion to rear-admiral. A sword used by Nelson at this time was an heirloom inherited from his uncle, Capt. Maurice Suckling, whose great-uncle, Admiral Galfridus Walpole, had carried it when he lost his arm commanding the 60-gunner *Lion* in 1711.

D2: Midshipman, 1797

A number of variations of midshipmen's coat are recorded; for example, a portrait of Midshipman Peter Downes (killed when the 52-gunner *Leander* was captured in August 1798) shows only six buttons on the coat breast, no blue line on the collar patch, and a double-breasted waistcoat. Guy Head's portrait of Nelson at Aboukir shows a blue 'frame' of piping around the button and loop on the collar patch, and buff trousers as depicted here. The Downes portrait shows a long dirk with straight quillons and spadroon-style hilt, on a black leather belt over the right shoulder, with an oval and apparently enamelled belt plate.

D3: Seaman, 1797

Wearing a typical costume, including straw hat and loose trousers, this seaman is equipped for boarding, with an unscabbarded cutlass thrust into his belt, and a boarding-pike. There being no distinctive uniform for seamen, to prevent confusion with an enemy dressed similarly, for boarding actions some manner of 'field-sign' might have been used. De Loutherbourg's painting of the cutting-out of the French ship *La Chevrette* in Cameret Bay in July 1801 by boarding parties from the British ships *Doris* (36 guns), *Beaulieu* (40), *Uranie* (38) and *Robust* (74) commanded by an officer from *Ville de Paris* (110), shows all except the uniformed marines wearing a white scarf or band tied around the upper arm, officers included.

D4: Private, 69th Foot, 1797

The 69th (South Lincolnshire) Regt. was deployed as marines from the start of the Revolutionary War, a detachment serving aboard the 74-gunner *Leviathan* at the 'Glorious First of June', and others under Nelson in both *Agamemnon* and *Captain*. Matthew Stevens of the 69th, who smashed the stern windows of *San Nicolas* and led the way for Nelson to the quarter-deck, rose to become paymaster of the 2/69th, in which capacity he served at Waterloo. Although closed lapels and a standing collar were introduced for infantry in 1796, this figure depicts the previous uniform as almost certainly worn at St. Vincent, with 'willow green' facings, and white lace with one red between two green stripes.

E1: Seaman, shore-going rig

Based upon a contemporary print, this shows a typical 'best uniform' worn for a trip ashore, including a jacket with white binding and large silver shoe buckles—evidence of plentiful prize-money. Robert Hay, who joined in 1803, described the walking-out dress as commonly including a dark blue jacket with pearl buttons, scarlet waistcoat bound with black ribbon, white trousers fringed at the ankle, pigtail to waist level, straw hat, a shark-bone cane under one arm, doxy under the other, plug of tobacco in the mouth and 'stingo' in the stomach, with the self-important air of an Indian nabob!

E2: Seaman, HMS Tribune, 1805

This figure is reconstructed from a description in *The Times*, October 1805, of a uniform apparently adopted by the crew of the 36-gun frigate *Tribune* (in service from 1803 until wrecked in 1839), perhaps at

Nelson wounded in the attack on Santa Cruz, Tenerife (where he lost his right arm); this engraving after R. Westall shows interesting marine 'campaign dress' including the long-tailed red coat with white facings, white trousers, lapels unfastened (figure at rear, holding boarding pike) and a battered 'round hat' (extreme left), perhaps a bicorn with the sides turned into a brim.

the behest of the captain. This vessel was known for 'the coxcombery of her crew... Every man wears a smart round Japan hat with green inside the leaf, a broad gold lace band, with the name of the ship painted in front in capital letters; black silk neckerchief, with a white flannel waistcoat bound with blue; and over it a blue jacket, with three rows of gold buttons very close together, and blue trousers'.

E3: Lieutenant, undress, c.1805

This shows the evolution in style from that of Plate B3, the hat now flat and worn 'fore-and-aft', the coat fastened across, with blue breeches and fashionable boots. This was more practical than the dress uniform, which one officer described as an 'absurd attire of tight white breeches and silk stockings, a fine open waistcoat, showing a yard of frill, with a neckcloth that took a particular man at least ten minutes to tie. Then there were brooches and buckles of all kinds, and I know not what other follies'. The sword is a naval version of the army 1803 flank company sabre, with a voided anchor in the guard.

E4: Officer, Royal Marines, c.1805

This shows the 'dress' version of the officers' uniform, with a laced coat instead of the unlaced version worn on service. Dighton shows this in his picture of Trafalgar, with the blue trousers depicted here instead of the white breeches and Hessian boots which might have been expected. Legwear specified in December 1805 was white breeches and long boots in summer, blue pantaloons and half-boots in winter.

F1: Vice-admiral, undress, 1805 (Horatio Nelson)

Based upon Scriven's engraving of Devis' portrait of Nelson, 'In the Dress he wore when he received his Mortal Wound', published in surgeon William Beatty's *Authentic Narrative* (London 1807), and upon the extant garment, this depiction of Nelson shows the 1795 regulation flag officers' undress. Nelson apparently wore an unlaced hat with a green shade which could be folded up or down, to shield his damaged right eye. His undress coat bore four embroidered stars: the Order of the Bath (top), the Order of St. Ferdinand and of Merit (Sicily, centre right), the Order of the Crescent (Ottoman, centre left), and the German Order of St. Joachim (bottom). Contrary to legend, no attempt was made to persuade Nelson to cover the decoration lest he attract the enemy's fire; surgeon Beatty and chaplain Dr. Scott discussed it, but knew Nelson so well that neither was prepared to risk his anger when they knew that the plea would be in vain.

F2: Vice-Admiral, full dress, 1805 (Cuthbert Collingwood)

Nelson's capable subordinate, who assumed command of the fleet after Nelson's death, is shown here in the 1795 regulation dress uniform. Giuseppe Politi's portrait painted in Sicily in 1807, the accuracy of which Collingwood confirmed, shows variations: ten lapel-loops (whereas William Owen's portrait, apparently not taken from life, appears to show eight); and instead of the correct two cuff-rings, Politi shows one, presumably the regulation being suffi-

Private of the Royal Marines in dress uniform; note the oval shoulder belt plate and the gaiters which appear to have no buttons but are perhaps laced on the outer seam. (Aquatint by I. C. Stadler after Charles Hamilton Smith, published in January 1815)

The landing at Aboukir, 8 March 1801: naval crews ready the boats as the troops disembark under fire. Note the carronade mounted in the prow of the nearest longboat. (Print after A. Dupray)

ciently ambiguous for the two rings of a vice-admiral to be taken as including the lace cuff-edging, instead of this being additional to the rank-rings. (Other portraits also show varying numbers of lapel-loops; Stuart's portrait of St. Vincent, for example, may indicate even more than ten.) The decorations shown here on the left lapel are the Naval Gold Medals for the 'Glorious First of June' and St. Vincent, worn on their white ribbon with blue edges in a typical manner.

F3: Captain, full dress, 1805 (Thomas Hardy)

This is based upon a portrait by Lemuel Abbott of Nelson's friend and assistant, Thomas Masterman Hardy, captain of HMS Victory at Trafalgar. The lapels are cut quite long, with ten loops each; and the cuff-lace shows a not uncommon design with pointed upper flap-lace. The regulations did not specify whether the two rows of cuff-lace applied to both cuff and flap; before 1787 the cuff had a single line and the flap two, but most evidence shows the 1795 cuff with a double row on each, perhaps originally an unofficial practice to distinguish captains from commanders.

F4: Private, Royal Marines, 1805

This marine sentry wears the post-1802 full uniform, with the white trousers shown in Denis Dighton's painting of Trafalgar. This uniform with white facings seems to have been worn from the adoption of the short-tailed, single-breasted infantry jacket until the implementation of the order which authorized blue facings.

G: Gun crew

Although four men could crew a gun, many more were required to haul on the ropes which, by means of blocks and tackle affixed to the ship's sides, pulled the gun inboard for loading and ran it out to fire through the gun-port. Elevation was by quoin, the wedge under the barrel; the barrel was lifted, and the carriage traversed, by handspikes. Ignition of the cannon by this date was by a flintlock mechanism bolted to the barrel immediately before action, primed by the gun-captain's powder horn as shown, and released by the gun-captain pulling a lanyard. This was very much safer than the earlier use of smouldering matches: HMS Queen Charlotte was burned in the Mediterranean in 1800, apparently by hay falling upon a burning match kept in a tub for the use of signal-guns. The flexible rammer, which had a length of cable instead of a shaft, meant that neither the gun had to be run so far inboard, nor had the gunner to lean out of the gun-port, in order to ram home the charge by the muzzle.

The typical costumes shown are based on several contemporary pictures, like Dighton's painting of Trafalgar. This shows a garment resembling a modern, long-sleeved, scoop-necked sweater, in various colours including hooped or striped; this may be the 'frock' noted as an alternative to shirts in a list of seamen's equipment for the sloop Pylades in 1814. Marines are described and depicted in contemporary sources as assisting the crewing of cannon; the man illustrated has removed his equipment and is wearing one of several recorded patterns of forage cap, an

'Landing Troops in the Face of the Enemy': a print by M. Dubourg after J. A. Atkinson. The seamen row the ships' boats ashore; a naval officer in the stern of the leading boat has a speaking trumpet to direct the landing of the following boats.

army-style folding cap with half-moon sides, as shown in a print of the bombardment of Algiers.

H1: Cook

Ships' cooks were appointed by warrant from the Commissioners of the Navy; all were Greenwich Pensioners, mostly ex-petty officers who had lost a limb on service. (A cook named Jennings is recorded as retiring only when he reached the age of 87, having spent 79 years in the navy). The position was largely a sinecure, as the only duty entailed soaking preserved meat to remove the salt, and then boiling it; the fat or 'slush' which floated to the top was the cook's perquisite, and though its sale was officially forbidden, it was in demand to spread upon the hard ship's biscuit. This figure is based upon an illustration by Rowlandson.

H2: Ship's boy

Admiralty regulations limited the number of boys employed on a ship, from 32 on a first-rater to 16 on a large frigate. They were usually supposed to act as officers' servants while learning seamanship, but some were put to seamen's duties immediately—hence the popular concept of the 'powder-monkey', boys who in action carried ammunition from the magazine to the guns.

H3: Carpenter

Each ship possessed a carpenter (a warrant officer) and one or two mates, plus a number of semi-skilled assistants; and each 'rated' ship had a caulker under the carpenter's orders, whose duty was to repair with oakum any damage to the caulking of the ship's sides and deck. This figure, after Rowlandson, wears a 'thrum cap', a cloth headdress made of 'thrums', fabric off-cuts woven to give a shaggy appearance.

H4: Boatswain's mate

This figure is based on a drawing by Edward Mangin, chaplain of the 74-gunner *Gloucester*. The hat bears a painted heraldic device (perhaps the captain's crest) and a scroll above with the name of the ship. The uniform includes what appears to be a white under-waistcoat with light blue laces, perhaps the 'inside jacket' mentioned in the list of seamen's equipment for the sloop *Pylades* in 1814, which also mentions both blue and white trousers for each man. The light blue laces may have been cords for the whistle or 'boatswain's call'. Responsible for enforcing discipline, boatswain's mates carried a 'starter' or 'rope's end', a length of rope with which to strike lazy seamen.

I1: Lieutenant, c.1810

This plate depicts members of a landing-party. The officer wears the dress jacket with lapels fastened over (taken from a portrait of c.1807–08), and the common white trousers; he is armed with a ship's pistol, dirk, and, as a more substantial weapon than the latter, an ordinary ship's cutlass.

I2: Master's mate, c.1810

This member of the second tier of warrant officers

wears the regulation coat with the standing collar introduced from 1807, worn open as depicted by Dighton, with a tall 'round hat' and blue trousers instead of the white breeches specified in 1787. He carries a simple type of hanger on a shoulder belt, and an ordinary ship's musket.

I3: Sergeant, Royal Marines, c.1810

Marine sergeants and corporals wore the old-style white knot on the right shoulder until chevrons were introduced as rank insignia, on the right arm, in September 1807; Dighton's picture of Trafalgar illustrates the later uniform. Sergeants had white lace, crimson sash with facing-coloured stripe, and initially carried halberds, like the army changing to spontoons, although this may not have occurred until as late as about 1797. An order of 6 May 1802 authorized sergeants to have yellow metal buttons and gold-laced hats instead of silver, implying that the latter had been in use, but this order was cancelled nine days later. Also in army style, corporals wore two sleeve chevrons, and the rank of colour sergeant was introduced in 1814 with a special badge, probably like that of the army.

I4: Seaman

An officer described the equipment of a landing-party at Java in 1811, when the 'Jacks' (seamen) were armed with a ship's cutlass apiece, 'a sort of straight iron-hoop-cut-in-lengths concern', and a ship's pistol, 'marvellously given to hanging fire . . . and, when it did go off, the ball, after divers girations in the ample barrel, generally flew kindly wide of any sort of harum-scarum aim taken by the sturdy possessor— if, perchance, any aim were taken at all'. All wore 'that marine Mambrino helmet', a tarred straw hat, and only the marines of the party carried muskets. They were accompanied by two light brass field-guns, but these refused to fire (*United Service Journal*, 1840). The cutlass shown here is supported in a leather shoulder belt, taken from an extant example.

J1: Master, c.1807

This illustrates the uniform of the senior warrant officers, regulated in 1787 and worn until 1807. The introduction in 1807 of a similar uniform but with standing collar may have been prompted by the somewhat civilian appearance of the original coat, which it was suggested had led to captured masters not being treated as officers. The old uniform continued in use for undress; that illustrated is based on a contemporary portrait, and includes a workman-like hanger on a shoulder belt.

'Landing Troops and Guns': a print after Thomas Rowlandson, 1801. The cannon are being hauled ashore by teams of seamen, while the gunners of the Royal Artillery (foreground) take their ease. In a number of operations the seamen remained ashore to help crew the guns.

J2: Surgeon, c.1807

Surgeons' 1805 full dress resembled that of physicians, without the lace but with chain embroidery on the collar, a single loop for ships' surgeons and two loops for those in shore hospitals. Undress was like that of physicians, minus the cuff- and pocket-buttons. This figure wears the fashionable white trousers in place of ordinary breeches.

J3: Seaman, landing party, Copenhagen, 1807

For the 1807 Copenhagen expedition the seamen who were to accompany marines for service ashore were ordered to wear blue jackets, white trousers and 'round hats', with a piece of canvas sewn to the right sleeve lettered with the name of their ship, to facilitate identification in case of 'straggling or misconduct'. Every man was to carry a haversack made from old canvas, with a spare shirt, pair of shoes and pair of stockings rolled up in a blanket. At the discretion of the commander they might be armed with muskets or pikes; the man illustrated has an ordinary ship's musket and bayonet.

J4: Officer, Royal Marines, c.1807

This shows the service uniform of marine officers, including an 'unlaced' coat with buttons in pairs (the collar-button is absent in one portrait) and lapels fastened across the breast; and a 'round hat' (as permitted for officers of the Plymouth Division as early as 1793), their feather plume noted in 1805 as rising 10 inches above the brim. For dress and probably on some other occasions they continued to wear the bicorn; an extant hat has the gold cockade-loop in a very wide 'V'. In June 1812 officers were ordered to wear the same hat as other ranks, and in October 1813 the 'ornament' (cockade loop?) on the front of officers' hats was abolished.

K1: Junior captain, c.1810

Plate K shows members of a captain's 'staff' who might have served aboard a frigate. This figure, based in part upon Edridge's 1807 portrait of Sir Thomas Foley, shows a typical dress uniform including white pantaloons and black-tasselled Hessian boots; the single epaulette identifies a captain of less than three years' post; a commander's uniform was identical, with the epaulette on the left. Some portraits show the turned-back 'triangles' of lapels cut in a somewhat exaggerated manner, for example in Northcote's 1804 portrait of Sir Edward Pellew Bt. as rear-admiral.

K2: Master

This Master wears the pre-1807 coat with falling collar as an undress garment, in preference to the 1807 dress coat which was similar but with a standing

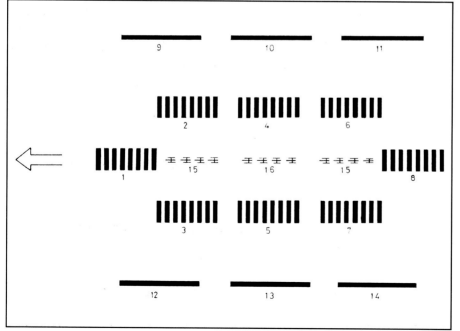

The utilization of seamen as troops: a plan of the order of march of the British forces which advanced on Capetown, 1795. Key: (1) Grenadier battalion (companies detached from the units present); (2) 95th Foot; (3) 98th Foot; (4) 78th Foot; (5) 84th Foot; (6) 1st Battn. Seamen; (7) 2nd Battn. Seamen; (8) battalion of marines; (9) 78th Light Company; (10) 95th Light Company; (11) St. Helena Light Company; (12) 84th Light Company; (13) 98th Light Company; (14) Light Company of seamen; (15) fieldpieces; (16) howitzers. Battalions marched in half companies in open order; the artillery was escorted by seamen armed with pikes; light infantry in open order on the flanks.

collar. Chaplain Mangin of HMS *Gloucester* pictured its Master in 1812 wearing a low 'round hat' and blue trousers as shown here, but with a non-regulation coat with 10 buttons on the single breast, apparently plain white cuffs, and shoulder-loops as on officers' undress coats, even though warrant officers wore no epaulettes.

K3: Midshipman

Although there were no regulation changes in midshipmen's uniform, the style changed gradually as with officers' coats; this typical uniform includes the common 'round hat', shown by Dighton with a gold loop on the left. A portrait of J. A. Allen, dated 1819, is similar to this, but shows more buttons on the breast (15), embroidered loops across the breast, and a bicorn. The very curved dirk was a fashion of the later years of the period.

K4: Volunteer

This youthful 'volunteer' or captain's servant, a relative or the offspring of a friend, is typical of the number of boys who served at sea to gain experience and the 'sea-time' necessary to allow them to sit for the lieutenancy promotion examination. Shown here is probably what was typical for a midshipman's undress uniform, which was unregulated, although the double-breasted coat might have a standing collar with white patch for midshipmen. Double-breasted blue jackets similar to those worn by seamen are recorded as early as 1780, probably often with three buttons on the cuff and, for midshipmen, the white collar patch.

L1: Vice-admiral, full dress, c.1813

Uniform amendments in March 1812 restored white facings for full dress. For flag officers, the coat had a blue collar and white lapels and cuffs, laced as before but with only a single band of gold lace on the upper edge of the cuff; with epaulettes as before, but with five, four, three and two cuff-rings respectively for admiral of the fleet, admiral, vice-admiral and rear-admiral. A crown was added above the anchor on the buttons. Undress was unchanged save for the new buttons, except for admiral of the fleet, whose coat was to have a blue collar and white lapels edged gold, white cuffs with five laces, and epaulettes as for full dress. Ultimately the lapels could be closed to resemble a white plastron (as shown in Beechey's portrait of Sir George Cockburn); but this style probably post-dated the Napoleonic Wars, the conventional manner of wearing the lapels being shown, e.g., in Joseph Slater's 1813 portrait of Gambier. Hats worn 'athwart' by this period were probably restricted to flag officers.

L2: Captain, full dress, c.1813

For captains and commanders the 1812 dress uniform was as before but with white cuffs and lapels, new buttons as for flag officers, and new epaulettes. All now wore two gold epaulettes, with plain straps for commanders, bearing a silver fouled anchor for captains of less than three years' post, and the same with a crown above for those of three years' post. Undress was as before, with new buttons and epaulettes. The figure illustrated, taken in part from Lane's portrait of Sir Philip Vere Broke, shows a

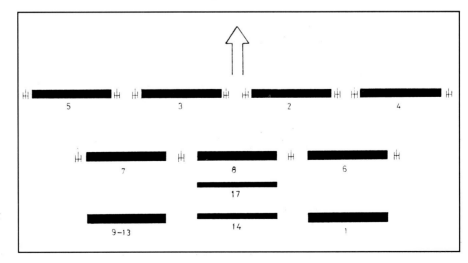

The order of battle for the force at the Cape; key as before, except that the light companies were concentrated into one light battalion, and the naval pikemen (17) were assembled in one body.

popular style of wearing the lapels partially fastened; and like L1 he carries the 1805 ornamented sword for commanders and above.

L3: Lieutenant, undress, c.1813

For lieutenants the 1812 dress uniform was like that of captains (including the adoption of three-button cuff-flap) but without lace, with new buttons, and a plain epaulette on the right shoulder only; undress was as before, with new buttons and the epaulettes. The figure illustrated wears two items common at sea; white trousers, and a plain 'round hat', often depicted as a wide-brimmed and low-crowned civilian-style headdress. A number of accounts record lieutenants wearing totally disreputable clothing at sea: Capt. Glascock described one in a worn-out coat, tarred nankeen trousers, a soup-stained buff waistcoat and a battered, broad-brimmed leather hat, the whole plastered with tar and whitewash.

L4: Boatswain

Following the restyling of warrant officers' dress uniform in 1807, involving the adoption of standing collars, use of the old coat was extended to lower-ranking personnel such as gunners, boatswains and carpenters. In other respects the clothing shown here is like that of an ordinary seaman, with the addition of the 'boatswain's call' whistle for signalling aboard ship.

Bibliography

Nelson's Navy: the Ships, Men and Organization 1793–1815, B. Lavery, London 1989, is the most comprehensive work on these aspects; *Life in Nelson's Navy*, D. Pope, London 1981, is an excellent account of organization and naval life; *Sea Life in Nelson's Time*, J. Masefield, 1905 (3rd edn., intro. C.C. Lloyd, London 1971) is still of value. *The Wooden World: An Anatomy of the Georgian Navy*, N.A.M. Rodger, London 1986, although concentrating on the Seven Years' War, is an excellent study with much of relevance. Among many works concerning ships and their equipment, *Sailing Ships of War 1400–1860*, Dr. F. Howard, London 1979; *The Arming and Fitting of English Ships of War 1600–1815*, B. Lavery, London 1987; and *The Line of Battle*, ed. R. Gardiner, London 1992, are very valuable. *Ships of the Royal Navy*, J.J. Colledge, New York 1969–70, is invaluable for identifying vessels and their 'rating'.

Naval uniforms and equipment are detailed in *British Naval Dress*, D. Jarrett, London 1960; *Uniforms of the Royal Navy during the Napoleonic Wars*, J. Mollo, London 1965 (officers only, but including marines); *The Dress of the British Sailor*, Admiral Sir Gerald Dickens, rev. edn. London 1977; *Uniforms of Trafalgar*, J. Fabb & J. Cassin-Scott, London 1977 (1805 period only); *Swords for Sea Service*, W.E. May & P.G.W. Annis, London 1970; *Naval Swords and Firearms*, W.E. May & A.N. Kennard, London 1962; and *Naval Swords: British and American Naval Edged Weapons, 1660–1815*, P.G.W. Annis, London 1970.

Just as the in-pensioners of the Royal Hospital at Chelsea had a uniform, so did those of the Naval Hospital at Greenwich, of which the domes of Wren's building are visible in the background. The uniform was somewhat archaic in style, including a plain bicorn, dark blue coat, waistcoat and breeches without decoration, and white stockings.

Histories of the Royal Marines include *Britain's Sea Soldiers*, Col. C. Field, Liverpool 1924; *The Royal Marines*, Maj.Gen. J.L. Moulton, London 1972; *The Royal Marine Artillery 1804–1923*, E. Fraser & L.C. Carr-Laughton, London 1930; and *Per Mare Per Terram: A History of the Royal Marines*, P.C. Smith, St. Ives 1974. *Royal Marines Records 1793–1836*, ed. A.J. Donald & J.D. Ladd, Royal Marines Historical Society, Eastney 1982, contains many interesting contemporary references.

Comparatively few photographs exist of naval personnel from the Napoleonic era. This is perhaps the most distinguished: Thomas Cochrane, 10th Earl of Dundonald (1775–1860), alias 'the Sea Wolf', the most audacious and successful of all British frigate captains, who served in a number of foreign navies after his unjust conviction for complicity in the great Stock Exchange fraud of 1814. He was eventually proven innocent and his rank in the Royal Navy was restored.

INDEX

(References to illustrations are shown in **bold**. Plates are shown with caption locators in brackets)